Y0-ABH-652

The
POLITICS of
BEING MORTAL

The
POLITICS of
BEING MORTAL

Alfred G. Killilea

THE UNIVERSITY PRESS OF KENTUCKY

Scholarly publisher for the Commonwealth,
serving Bellarmine College, Berea College, Centre
College of Kentucky, Eastern Kentucky University,
The Filson Club, Georgetown College, Kentucky
Historical Society, Kentucky State University,
Morehead State University, Murray State University,
Northern Kentucky University, Transylvania University,
University of Kentucky, University of Louisville,
and Western Kentucky University.

Editorial and Sales Offices: Lexington, Kentucky 40506-0336

Library of Congress Cataloging-in-Publication Data
Killilea, Alfred G., 1941-
    The politics of being mortal / Alfred G. Killilea.
        p.   cm.
    Bibliography: p.
    Includes index.
    ISBN 0-8131-1643-0 (alk. paper)
    1. Death—Social aspects—United States.   2. Death—Political
aspects—United States.   3. Social values.   I. Title.
HQ1073.5.U6K55   1988
306.9—dc19   88-9422

This book is printed on acid-free paper meeting the
requirements of the American National Standard for
Permanence of Paper for Printed Library Materials. ∞

To my daughter, MARI
November 21, 1970 - October 26, 1987

You taught me pure joy in play,
the diligence behind achievement,
and finally the full depth of the human condition.

Contents

Acknowledgments

My ideas in this work have been prompted and nurtured by countless benefactors. Academic mentors who were especially important include Richard Giannone, Edward Goerner, Joseph Evans, and Ernest Bartell at the University of Notre Dame and the late Herbert Storing at the University of Chicago. Colleagues at the University of Rhode Island who read the manuscript at various stages and gave valuable advice include Norman and Naomi Zucker, Lawrence Rothstein, Arthur Stein, Galen Johnson, Yvette Mintzer, and Robert and Gerry Tyler. Michael Vocino assisted in both research and morale.

I am indebted to a vast number of students who pondered and helped to refine the ideas in this book, especially Simon Pressman, Marisa Quinn, and Robert Hackey, who were students in my seminar on death and politics. I am grateful to the University of Rhode Island for several research grants in support of this book and to William R. Ferrante, vice president for academic affairs, and my late dean, Barry A. Marks, for their confidence in my work.

This book could simply not have been completed without the extraordinary secretarial help of Sharon Woodmansee and Joanne Walsh. Their alchemy that turned dishevelled pages into polished copy was a gift I can never reciprocate. The same may be said of the superb editing work of Evalin F. Douglas of the University Press of Kentucky.

In learning to deal with the subject of death I feel a very personal debt to Gail O'Brien, Fredrika Schweers, Gavin Knott, Peter Findlay, and Rose Pressman. This book is a culmination of encouragement I received from Addie Killilea and of the lifelong education and love received from my parents, Frank and Isabel. My wife, Mary Ann, and my children, Joe and Mari, were my most constant source of insight, reassurance, and humor throughout the writing of this book.

1. Death as a Paradox

I don't mind the idea of dying. I just don't want to be
there when it happens.

—Woody Allen

This book about death is more about life and how facing the
fact of our mortality can allow us to live with less anxiety, more
freedom. In exploring the possible rewards of a greater acceptance of death in society, I will examine implications of Paul
Tillich's question: "If we cannot accept death, can we really
live?" Throughout, I will deal in various ways with one central
irony: whereas the subject of death has been avoided in our
culture lest it rob life of meaning and contentment, confronting death may be crucial for us, individually and as a society, to
affirm life and even, in the nuclear age, to survive.

In the last two decades, significant developments have begun to challenge our culture's denial of death. These include
the burgeoning literature on death and dying, the hospice
movement, greater frankness of physicians in discussing
death, the demand for organ donation, and, of most significance, a growing awareness of the immense peril that the
world faces in the nuclear arms race. These developments
provoke questions about the changes society would undergo if
the subject of death were let out of the closet, yet the treatment
of death in our culture remains one of denial.

This denial is sometimes self-conscious and elaborate, as in
the cryogenic freezing of bodies to be rehabilitated in the
future, or the "tasteful" services at the Forest Lawn Cemetery
Chapel, or the assigning of death and dying to professionals in
nursing homes, hospitals, and funeral homes. Geoffrey Gorer
has summarized our culture's attitude toward mortality by
pointing to "the pornography of death." He argues that where-

as our Victorian predecessors regarded death as a regular, frequent part of life but treated sex with delicacy and denial, magically finding babies under cabbages, we are casual and cavalier about sex but treat death with avoidance and magical explanations.[1]

Our avoidance of death is not always in word. We sometimes talk about death in a metaphoric and unthreatening context as if to convince ourselves that death need not be intimidating. The terminology of sports, which represents one of the major preoccupations in our culture, is full of references to death. We speak of runners "dying on base," of a batter getting a "new life," and of games ending in "sudden death." These metaphors on one level seem to disarm death, to trivialize it, for we know that there is life after sudden death in athletics.

An important part of our absorption in spectator sports, reflected by billions of dollars in television revenues, may be traced to the image of control and mastery that exquisite athletic expertise conveys. An artfully executed touchdown pass can be appreciated for its beauty and skill, but it is also an invitation to hope that this triumph is a figure of control over the uncertainties and ambiguities that being mortal imposes upon us. Sports free us from ambiguities: every event is autopsied with endless statistics; the final figures on the scoreboard are what count regardless of which team has actually played better; referees never reconsider judgment calls; and everyone hates a tie. Sports function as a release from many of life's pressures, but the effort to relieve the uncertainty and threat of the mortality we seldom consciously confront may be one of sports' chief missions.

Because Americans do break the taboo against speaking about death, whether in discussing sports, crimes, or war, some question whether we do not give death's reality its due. Our avoidance of death is not total, but one would have to ignore a vast part of our culture to miss the extraordinary lengths to which we go to hide from death. Among empirical studies of our avoidance, A.E. Christ's shows that 87 percent of a population of acute geriatric patients never discussed death or dying; and Richard Kalish's studies document how much slower hospital nurses were in responding to the call lights of terminal patients as opposed to nonterminal patients.[2] But the modern avoidance of death is even more convincingly described in a comprehensive evaluation by historian Philippe Aries.

Aries describes this century's treatment of death in Western culture, aside from the rather sudden increase of studies in the last twenty years, as one of silence: "It is strange how the human sciences, so outspoken regarding family, work, politics, leisure, religion, and sex, have been so reserved on the subject of death. Scholars have kept silent. . . . Their silence is only a part of this great silence that has settled on the subject of death in the 20th century."[3] He indicts Western society in this century for depriving the dying person of his or her death. In earlier times, a patient "insisted on participating in his own death, because he saw in his death the moment when his individuality received its ultimate form." The patient "was master over his life only insofar as he was master over his death" (139). The deathbed was the place and time at which last spoken wishes became sacred to the survivors: "For his part, the dying man was satisfied that he could rest in peace on the word of his close ones. This trust that began in the seventeenth and eighteenth centuries and was developed in the nineteenth century, has in the twentieth turned into alienation. As soon as serious danger threatens one member of a family, the family immediately conspires to deprive him of information and thus his freedom" (140).

Physicians, until recently, were a key part of this conspiracy of silence, and many still are. Until the twentieth century, Aries notes, medical ethics made it obligatory to inform patients of their conditions. "A papal document of the Middle Ages made this a task of the doctor, a task he for a long time carried out unflinchingly" (136-37).

Where the modern physician has left off in the denial of death, the funeral industry has taken over. Jessica Mitford, among others, details how American funeral customs mask the reality of death. Featured among a selection of caskets are those made of solid copper—"a quality casket which offers superb value to the client seeking long-lasting protection." Casket manufacturers like Elgin offer a "perfect posture bed" or a Colonial Classic line with some caskets "equipped with foam rubber, some with inner spring mattresses." Richard Dumont and Dennis Foss describe the funeral industry's "willing compliance with the public's desire to make the corpse appear to be quite alive."[4]

To some extent, the avoidance of death simply fits the American national experience. Ours is a young country unencrusted by traditions and unimpressed by genealogy charts. Preoccupied with pushing back frontiers, we learned to value heartiness and self-reliance. Old age and death have seemed unAmerican from the start on a continent that demanded and rewarded belief in possibilities rather than an appreciation of limits. A people who found it expedient to expropriate the lands of Native Americans would not be likely to dwell on the debts of one generation to another. A nation so profusely, almost profligately, endowed by nature in its geography has found little time to be attentive to nature's control of the life span.

Our mindset to see nature not so much as a tutor but as a challenge has led us to extraordinary heights of technological achievement. This dominance in technology has been abetted by our not being strapped to tradition or constraints in the market of ideas and investments. The challenge of technological development in this century helped to maintain the frontier mentality long after the geographic frontier was gone.

Inevitably, with so much of our national history reinforcing a belief in progress, death became for us not a natural and necessary part of life but an embarrassment, a rebuke to our faith in the future. For many, death represented just another obstacle to conquer or, at the very least, to avoid with grace and pretense. The fight to defeat cancer, for example, represents for some a campaign against death. Sociologist Robert Blauner summarizes this clash of values in observing that "the dead and their concerns are simply not relevant to the living in a society that feels liberated from the authority of the past and orients its energies toward immediate preoccupations and future possibilities."[5]

John Stephenson agrees that "death is antithetical to the American image of what is important in life." He says death represents failure to us, failure of science and failure of the individual, who is supposed to be master of his or her own fate. The stasis that characterizes death clashes with the American ideal of progress and activity. "There is, as a result, a tinge of guilt upon the state of being dead in America."[5] Stephenson echoes the theme of "death as pornography" that was first raised thirty years before by Gorer: "And so we react to the reality of death with dread. The subject is obscene; it is pornographic. It is not polite to speak easily of death. We are too uncomfortable with it. Institutions are created to contain death, and emphasis is placed upon youth, for to grow old is to exemplify the decay of the body."[6]

Stephenson's treatment of the theme of death as pornography provides an excellent answer to those who ask how it can be alleged that our culture shuns death when death is a constant theme on television and in news reports. Some of this public acknowledgment should be taken at face value as an indication that the denial of death, although pervasive, is not universal in society. Robert Kastenbaum and Ruth Aisenberg observe that one factor driving the new surge of interest in death is that with television we are less isolated from violent death, as was certainly the case during the Vietnam War.[7]

Stephenson, however, convincingly argues that much of our public treatment of death actually confirms the link to pornography. With help from Gorer, he deepens the parallel between the Victorian treatment of sexuality and contemporary death attitudes: "The repression of sexuality brought with it a flourishing of pornography. The attempt to deny the existence of death by repressing the subject has brought about a popular fascination with violence. The similarities go further. As with sexual pornography, the pornography of violent death de-emphasizes feelings. . . . In sexual pornography there is little or no caring, tenderness, or love. In necrography (violent pornography), people are 'wasted' or 'blown away.' The emphasis in both cases is upon the sensational." Necrography, he tells us, serves as a form of substitute gratification, "allowing us to meet death and remain unscathed, and our feelings of grief and mourning are replaced by the thrill of pseudo-terror at the violent act" (40).

Thus much of the overt image of death in our society is part of our denial. We continue to hide from the reality of our natural and unavoidable mortality by exposing ourselves to the more bizarre and violent manifestations of death. As Stephenson puts it, "authentic presentations of taboo subjects are prohibited, but more indirect (and perhaps perverse) presentations are acceptable" (40). Also, Kastenbaum and Aisenberg remind us that "overemphasis upon accidental fatalities is a way of reinforcing our belief that death is some place else." Death is seen as an external act that may befall us but is not within ourselves. They suggest the notion of death as accidental can be interpreted as an inclination to remain within the child's universe of causality. "Children tend to see death threats as being closely related to concrete circumstances. Avoid those circumstances and one avoids death" (200).

A final distinction needs to be made in perceiving the avoidance of death in American culture. While observing that "the overwhelming majority of investigators argue that Americans seek to evade death," Stephenson notes that if the denial were total, chaos would develop when death occurred. Therefore we are ambivalent toward death: "we both deny and accept death—we deny when we can, and accept when we must." We need, he concludes, to distinguish between *extrinsic death*—the death represented by mortality tables and statements such as "all living things must die"—and *existential death*, which refers to our personal death. It is primarily existential death against which contemporary men and women are "bereft of any symbolic or theological armament," Stephenson says: "From earliest childhood on, we are taught not to think of death; to do so is morbid and unacceptable. As a result, we numb ourselves to death's existence, allowing it into our consciousness only as distant, nonthreatening, abstract death. . . . Our internal confusion and lack of symbolic referents for the reality of personal death [lead] us to defensive actions, such as avoidance, in order to deal with it" (43-44).

On the other hand, the growth of life insurance sales and pre-need funeral plans evidence that "on some levels extrinsic death is affirmed by Americans" (44). This dualistic nature of our reactions to death, as emphasized by Stephenson, is a crucial part of a response to those who question whether Americans avoid the subject. Our culture does allow such discussion, but it tends to be about the abstract, nonthreatening, extrinsic sides of death. Taboos against discussing personal death are under attack by many but remain prevalent in our society.

However, whether we like it or not, whether we face it or not, we live always in death's presence. We strive for "normalcy" by assigning goals to our lives that seem to skirt death's significance. Our economy constantly goads us in a quest for more, as if that were all that life is for. But though we laugh at the few heroic neurotics like Woody Allen who keep pushing death on our consciousness, we can never fully insulate ourselves from stories of what happens to others. We seek out details about those singled out by death in the hope that we don't know them, in the hope that if they have no connection to us they do not signal our connection to death and vulnerability. But sooner or later we realize that nothing separates us from others who are touched by death, and, sooner or later, we will be touched as well.

The tragedy of the January 1986 explosion of the space shuttle *Challenger* reached almost inconsolable depths throughout the United States because it was totally unexpected and because the crew included a bright, effervescent teacher and mother who represented the public as the first private citizen in space. When, within an instant on live television, what was to be a glorious, fortunate flight for someone selected from among thousands and with whom we were proud to identify, was terminated by accident, error, fate, death, we knew we had no place to hide.

The great irony of our effort to hide from death and human

vulnerability is not that it is so unavailing, but that we would be miserable if we succeeded. Only in confronting human mortality can we appreciate the limitedness and the preciousness of life. It is not death we fear as much as it is annihilation and the absurdity of a meaningless life. The paradox of death is that it is a spur to put aside the inducements we have all around us for a meaningless life and to find significance and permanence in the effect we have upon other people's lives. Nothing confirms our identity with other mortals and our mutual dependence as powerfully as death does. Death visits us with great grief and pain, but it also highlights our connection with all other people and the power we have to continue life in others.

Since this perspective is the key insight pursued throughout this book, it is obvious that this book is about change as well as death. The acceptance of death argued for here is not limited to a religious view. Many people assume that it is impossible to confront death without the support of religion, and that those who are not religious must necessarily be cynical or shallow. Ernest Becker declares that "since there is no secular way to resolve the primal mystery of life and death, all secular societies are lies." Glenn Tinder seems to agree: "If a person is not immortal, he tends to sink back into nature and in some circumstances may be regarded, like any other natural being, as a means rather than an end." These philosophical doubts about how serious secular people can be about death and life have a significant political impact. In one of his first interviews after taking office in January 1981, President Ronald Reagan said that one reason there was little hope for common understanding between the United States and the Soviets is that "they don't believe in after-life."[8]

The fact that so many churches in America participate in death-denying funeral customs, like concluding the graveside service before burial, suggests that difficulty in coping with death is not confined to secular people. Surely one important factor behind the appeal of cults and some fundamentalist sects is the simple, almost automatic victory over death they hold out. But this escape from the pressures of mortality and vulnerability is accompanied by an abandonment of reason and an irresponsible indifference to moderation in the face of a nuclear Armageddon. If ever it were important to see how mortality can be confronted and accepted on purely human terms, this is such a time. This book supports those people— secular and religious—who reject the self-interested approach to God as an escape from death and who see dignity and unity in people simply because they share the gift of life. If death is seen as confirming, rather than threatening, this dignity and unity, then a greater acceptance of death in our culture should have a powerful impact on our social, political, and religious attitudes.

The effort to promote greater democracy would be vigorously advanced by a less defensive response to death, for acknowledging our common mortality seems to be a catalyst to taking equality and community more seriously. Likewise, business as usual in our economic life would be challenged, for the incentive of merely getting "more" would not hold up against the lessons death teaches about limits in life and the need to set priorities. The ballooning of one's ego by manic acquisition is pricked by candor about death.

The issue where changed attitudes about death have their most significant and urgent impact is the crisis we face in the nuclear arms race. Perhaps a major reason so many of us are oblivious to the danger of nuclear war and have given policy makers such a free hand in rattling nuclear sabers since Hiroshima is that we strive to be oblivious to death. If we were to confront our mortality and realize that our life has a permanence and value in our ability to give life to others in the long chain of human interaction, we would realize what an unspeakable crime against the future is represented by the threat of nuclear war. We would give our policy makers a very short leash in their maneuvering of the arms race, and we would evidence a popular consciousness on this issue previously not thought possible.

Of course, this consciousness has already begun to form. Even while reaffirming his description of the Soviet Union as an "evil empire," President Reagan negotiated significant cuts in our missile arsenal. To the extent that the increasing public pressure for movement away from nuclear confrontation has been spurred by the immensity of the crisis rather than by new attitudes about death, we can see how these two changes are mutually reinforcing. People who take seriously the threat of nuclear arms must necessarily transcend the denial of death and begin to gain some perspective on their individual deaths. At the very least, they will realize how minor their deaths are compared to the death of all humanity. Concern for human life in any context may begin in self-interest, but it never ends there; a concern for protecting humanity against nuclear arms engenders the attitudes and values that support people in accepting their individual deaths.

The kinds of changes this book explores—greater participation in our politics, less self-interested appeals in our economy, greater concern for the reality of nuclear peril in our national security policies—are large and momentous, but so are the provocations to these changes. Since in the nuclear age, for the first time in human history, we have the power to put an end to life on this planet, why should we be surprised that humanity might now develop a new consciousness about interdependence and the necessity to restrain nationalism and individual ego in order to survive? On the personal level, as we realize the price we pay in unreality and insecurity for the denial of death, why should we be surprised that people will refuse to devote their lives to a preoccupation with wealth and power?

Even without the urgency about change that nuclear weapons force upon us, can we not expect that the emptiness of spending a life trying to impress others or even oneself, particularly when it is done to ward off intimations of mortality, will increasingly arouse people's demand for meaning in life? With the urgency for new priorities in the nuclear era glaring at us and with the personal need to deal with death in order to deal honestly with life, we begin to realize that we are living at a time when the status quo is no longer an option. We will as a society either harden ourselves to the nuclear peril we face and buttress this choice with greater nationalism, greater arms, greater danger, or we will seek out the basis for human soli-

darity and act to save our common world. We will, as individuals, either spend our lives running from death and seek a lonely
and futile refuge in narcissism, or we will acknowledge our
limits and restructure our priorities with a new appreciation
of life's preciousness and our power to share life with others.
On both societal and personal levels, if we choose to face
reality we will find that accepting our mortality and vulnerability will be our most valuable aid in moving to greater
solidarity and harmony with other cultures and persons.

In uncovering the irony of how acknowledging our mortality does not rob life of meaning but rather prompts us to
find meaning in life, this book will first consider and respond
to the arguments of Ernest Becker and Jacques Choron that the
denial of death is natural and inevitable. The third chapter will
examine the case presented by Robert Jay Lifton that, whereas
there are modes of immortality that liberate us from the denial
of death, these modes are rendered impotent by the threat of
nuclear war. The fourth chapter is the linchpin for the whole
book, for it will lay out the ways by which we can accept death
without a dependence upon, but not necessarily in opposition
to, religious beliefs. The focus of this chapter is on how our
impact on other people's lives is not negated by the grief and
suffering that are the companions of death and how this impact assures meaning in life.

In the first of four chapters on the political and social results
of a great acceptance of death in our culture, chapter five
argues that there is a serious collision between the respect for
limits that death teaches and the encouragement in capitalism
to acquire more and more. In exploring this clash, chapters
five and six examine the ideas of John Locke, Michael Novak,
Daniel Bell, and Christopher Lasch. Chapter seven looks at the
implications of a new perspective on death for the prospect of
greater participatory democracy in our society. Confronting
our mortality is seen here to have great force as a catalyst to
finding shared values in a pluralistic society. Chapter eight
confronts and tests the treatment of death and life in this book
with the awesome peril of nuclear war. Building on a helpful

but incomplete foundation laid by Johnathan Schell, this chapter sees the acceptance of personal death as a powerful motivation to action against nuclear death. The conclusion reemphasizes how accepting death directly conflicts with and undermines economic and political appeals based on a narrow concept of self-interest. Mirroring the paradoxes that run throughout this book, our greatest self-interest—to live freely without the pervasive anxiety that death threatens us with extinction and absurdity—is seen to be achievable only by a commitment to the common interest and a mutual sharing of life with other people. It is in this respect that this book about death necessarily becomes a study of our capacity for living.

2. Surmounting the Denial of Death

> No philosophy, religion, or overall way of life can be
> judged complete or adequate unless it includes a
> definite position on whether or not the human
> personality can surmount the crisis called death.
> —Corliss Lamont

More open attitudes toward death in our society can serve as a catalyst for a wider acceptance of the social values of equality and community. This proposition is shared by several authors who have weighed the social impact of people coming to terms with their mortality. Herman Feifel has argued that an acceptance of death would lessen the need to project the fear of death outside ourselves and would mute some of the violence of our times, "perhaps even fortifying man's gift for creative splendor against his genius for destruction." Corliss Lamont also emphasizes the social implications of changing attitudes toward death: "The social meaning of death . . . has its positive aspects. For the occurrence of death brings home to us the common concerns and the common destiny of all men everywhere. It draws us together in the deep-felt emotions of the heart and dramatically accents the ultimate equality involved in our ultimate fate. The universality of death reminds us of the essential brotherhood of man that lies beneath all the bitter dissensions and conflicts registered in history and contemporary affairs."[1]

Similar arguments about the social repercussions of the consciousness of death are made by Charles Wahl, Peter Koestenbaum, Leon Kass, Norman Cousins, H. Tristham Englehardt, and Robert Jay Lifton.[2] First, however, we need to consider why so many more social scientists and theorists on politics remain under the sway of La Rochefoucauld's contention that human beings "cannot look directly at either the sun or death." These writers argue that the avoidance of the subject of death is both natural and necessary.

In spite of the dramatic movement in the last two decades to reverse the shunning of death in our culture, this movement is vigorously challenged by the insistence that the only alternative to a religious belief in immortality is a firm and pervasive denial of death. This argument is made with special intensity by theologians, of whom Paul Ramsey is perhaps the best-known representative. Ramsey scoffs at the effort to speak of death with dignity and insists that death is not natural to human life and that "a true humanism and the dread of death seem to be dependent variables."[3] He sees no philosophical basis for a secular acceptance of death and assumes that a movement aimed at such a goal avoids the denial of death only by emasculating death's reality and tragedy: "To deny the indignity of death requires that the dignity of man be refused also. The more acceptable in itself death is, the less the worth or uniqueness ascribed to the dying life" (90).

The obstacles to facing death without the consolation of the promise of spiritual immortality are equally imposing to other authors. Vivian Rakoff wonders if the belief in an afterlife may not be the only way to allay "primordial anguish." William F. May believes people "evade death because they recognize in the event an immensity that towers above their resources for handling it." Robert Fulton and Gilbert Geis see the increasing tendency in contemporary society to assign to professional functionaries the responsibility for traditional family roles regarding the dead as permitting us "to avoid close and disturbing confrontations with the inconsistencies inherent in the traditional theological explanations and the emerging secular viewpoints." A critic of these attitudes, Yeager Hudson, notes the "quiet desperation" in many lives totally intimidated by death unsoftened by religion. For many, "the bleak fact of death has given rise to a hedonistic attitude which amounts to an attempt to wring out of our few brief days such pleasure as they may be made to yield." These attitudes, he concludes, "seem to presuppose that no matter how good a man's life is, unless it is eternal it is in the final evaluation dust and ashes."[4]

The conviction that the consciousness of death is not tolerable for the nonreligious receives its most scholarly recent support from French philosopher Jacques Choron. More than any other author on the subject in the last twenty years, he has given to the study of attitudes toward death a philosophical depth and comprehensive analysis. His two major works, *Death and Western Thought* and *Death and Modern Man*, examine the difficulty Western philosophy has had since the Renaissance in giving meaning to life in the shadow of death. Especially in the latter book, largely composed of Choron's commentaries on arguments of major philosophers summarized in the former work, he comes reluctantly but firmly to the conclusion that, on its own terms, life seems an enigma that denies perspective and significance.

Early in *Death and Modern Man*, Choron identifies the core of the human dilemma as stemming not from the fear of death but the fear of extinction: "It is the prospect of not being anymore that makes most men abhor death."[5] The conviction expressed by Shelley and echoed by poets and philosophers throughout Choron's book that "there is something in man at enmity with nothingness and dissolution" (80) leads Choron to review what he considers the most important attempts to uncover the meaning of life. He first criticizes the position that the purpose of life is to be found in "growth and self-fulfillment, the achievement of emotional maturity, of moral stature, and of intellectual excellence, the becoming a 'rounded personality.'" He also argues that "no matter how desirable these are in themselves none of them can be the *ultimate* meaning of life as long as it is not related to something enduring but remains an end in itself and not a means to a higher end" (171). It is clear that, for Choron, "endurance" is an essential precondition for life or its activities to have meaning. For this reason, he finds even the life "spent in the pursuit of goodness and beauty" vulnerable to W.W. Dixon's despair: "If, indeed, existence offers any values it can only be to the individual beings who have a share in existence. If there be any good, and if there be any beauty it is in them and their perceptions of such things. Where else could it be? The rest is but mud and motion. And since if the valuators perish, all values, truth, goodness and the rest, go with them into everlasting night, no theological or metaphysical twitterings can rebut the demonstrable hollowness of life, its inherent futility" (172).

The inability to find meaning in some enduring dimension to life leads Choron to bleak language in this dispassionate treatise: "The death of the good and wise, when moral character and spiritual greatness, painfully acquired through the years, disappear like smoke, only underscores the absurdity of death and the futility of all human striving" (172). One hears the echo in this search for meaning in the face of annihilation of Ecclesiastes ("Time and chance happeneth to them all") and the long-standing warning in Christian contemplative writing about the "vanity of vanities." James Joyce could not have portrayed more poignantly the melancholy of secularism that was denounced by his Jesuit educators.

Choron next considers the argument that "loving and being loved constitute the meaning of life." But like Freud in *Civilization and Its Discontents*, Choron quickly focuses on the heightened vulnerability of lovers to what Shakespeare described as "love-destroying death." Choron is impressed by the biological effect of love at least to limit death's power; he finds that "to have progeny is possibly the only meaning of life." But he convincingly rejects biological immortality as the answer to the meaning of life because "there are too many 'absurd' deaths left": those who are childless or who die in their youth. For the same reason, he rejects the claim that the meaning of life can be found in creative work. "Can we accept as an answer to the meaning of life that which can be applicable only to a few privileged individuals? Even with these persons there is no question that their creations, although often spoken of as 'immortal,' are not everlasting" (172-73).

Again, we see that Choron's critical criterion for finding meaning in the face of death is endurance beyond death and time. It is almost by necessity that he finds humanity a victim of "the melancholy truth of the perishability of all that the skill of human hands and the flight of human spirit has brought forth." His rejection of the final, and perhaps most common, claim for transcendent significance in life—contributing to humanity—seems inevitable:

Even "serving causes," making one's country or the world "a better place to live in" by striving to eliminate suffering and injustice and preserve peace—in spite of being the loftiest goals mortal man can strive for—cannot be considered as an answer to the question of the ultimate meaning of life. For it is not enough that the "cause" be outside of the individual human life; it must also be "above mankind." And this—because of the possibility, and perhaps even the inevitability, of eventual cessation not only of Western civilization, but of all life on the planet, and the disintegration of the earth itself—becomes a doubtful possibility. [174]

The cumulative effect of Choron's denial of the efficacy of these attempts at consolation and meaning in the path of annihilating death is to give reluctant but vigorous support to the proposition that the denial of death in our secular culture is not an aberration. It is the only straw left at which one can grab to avoid the numbing sting of awareness of impending oblivion. That this should be the conclusion of a writer with Choron's composure and scholarship is a formidable challenge to those who would argue that death-denying behavior in our society is both pathological and unnecessary and that the confrontation and ultimate acceptance of death is not only possible but portends vast changes in the quality of life in society.

This challenge also finds substantial and spirited reinforcement in the recent work of Ernest Becker. If Choron's is the most scholarly of contemporary studies on the inevitability of the denial of death, Becker's last two books are clearly the most startling and dramatic in their presentation of this theme and in sketching its far-reaching implications for the individual and for society. His extraordinary pessimism about the possibility of finding either equanimity or meaning in the face of human mortality was detailed in 1973 in his Pulitzer Prize-winning *The Denial of Death*. The equally bleak social reper-cussions of this view were described in *Escape from Evil*, pub-lished in 1975 just after Becker's death.

Becker sees people as having no choice but to deny death because they are hopelessly caught in the dilemma of having magnificent illusions of power in a decaying, vulnerable body. He is simply awed by how completely and miserably the human animal, from infancy on, is undercut in its narcissistic sense of magical omnipotence, uniqueness, and creativity by the absurdity of mortality:

This is the paradox: he is out of nature and hopelessly in it; he is dual, up in the stars and yet housed in a heart-pumping, breathgasping body that once belonged to a fish and still carries the gillmarks to prove it. His body is a material and fleshy casing that is alien to him in many ways—the strangest and most repugnant way being that it aches and bleeds and will decay and die. Man is literally split in two: he has an awareness of his own splendid uniqueness in that he sticks out of nature with a towering majesty, and yet he goes back into the ground a few feet in order blindly and dumbly to rot and disappear forever. It is a terrifying dilemma to be in and to have to live with.[6]

So grotesque is the human fate of consciousness of both one's symbolic self, "a creature with a name, a life history," and one's "fundamental expendability in nature" (52), that Becker is convinced "a full apprehension of man's condition would drive him insane" (27). The only way around the terror of death and the absurd dualism of life and death is to deny mortality, and thus "man lives by lying to himself about himself and about his world" (51). Rather than breeding anxiety and thwarting a reconciliation with nature and other people, as some claim, the denial of death is the prime requirement of the conviction that "the individual has to repress *globally*, from the entire spectrum of his experience, if he wants to feel a warm sense of inner value and basic security" (52).

The psychological urgency of denying death leads necessari-ly to a rejection of the advice from Abraham Maslow and others about "enjoying one's full humanness." As Becker sees it, a therapeutic enterprise that encourages honesty about the lies that are essential for sanity leads to a Pyrrhic victory: "The person gives up something restricting and illusory, it is true, but only to come face to face with something even more awful: genuine despair. Full humanness means full fear and trembling, at least some of the waking day. When you get a person to emerge into life, away from his dependencies, his automatic safety in the cloak of someone else's power, what joy can you promise him with the burden of his aloneness? . . . What would the average man do with a full consciousness of absurdity?" (59).

These provocative ideas and strong language, drawn from *The Denial of Death*, lead directly to *Escape from Evil* and its equally stark explanation of the social and political effects of each person's harrowing dualism. Becker's argument gives vigorous support to the much-neglected relevance to political attitudes of attitudes toward death. Unfortunately, this connection is not a happy one for the democratic ideals of liberty and equality. Precisely because people cannot tolerate the dualism of life and death discussed in *The Denial of Death*, they cannot tolerate freedom. They are quite prepared, Becker argues, to leave a political freedom that offers no protection against the bondage of mortality and to gather in the shadow of a forceful leader whose power in human events symbolizes a power against the great enemy, death.

Becker is not alone in this posture. Against the optimistic assumptions of primitive equality and liberty encased in Rousseau's famous dictum that "Man was born free, and everywhere he is in chains," Becker's mentor, Otto Rank, had insisted that "every human being is also equally unfree, that is we are born in need of authority and we even create out of freedom a prison." And in *Life Against Death*, Norman O. Brown had argued: "If there is a class which has nothing to lose but its chains, the chains that bind are self-imposed, sacred obligations which appear as objective realities with all the force of a neurotic delusion." Becker weaves these earlier arguments in support of his central proposition that "men fashion unfreedom as a bribe for self-perpetuation" and to support the inference that such effort is necessary because death is an idea with which it is not possible to cope.[7]

Becker qualifies Choron's description of the great human fear as the fear of extinction and describes it as the fear of "*extinction with insignificance.*" The job of any culture thus becomes a sacred and religious one: to assure in some way the perpetuation of its members. Culture must "raise men above nature, to assure them that in some ways their lives count in the universe more than merely physical things count" (4).

Becker is convinced, however, that this mission of all cultures is doomed to failure and that the symbolic denial of mortality is "a figment of the imagination for flesh-and-blood organisms" (85). Since the terror of death remains underneath the cultural repression, the fear of death is shifted to the higher level of cultural perpetuity, and with disastrous consequences:

Since men must now hold for dear life onto the self-transcending meanings of the society in which they live, onto the immortality symbols which guarantee them indefinite duration of some kind, a new kind of instability and anxiety [is] created. And this anxiety is precisely what spills over into the affairs of men. In seeking to avoid evil, man is responsible for bringing more evil into the world than organisms could ever do merely by exercising their digestive tracts. It is man's ingenuity, rather than his animal nature, that has given his fellow creatures such a bitter earthly fate. [5]

The unhappy consequences of people's inability to accept their mortality are particularly apparent for Becker in the way we treat competition and wealth: "importance equals durability equals life" (13). This simple formula, he says, locks us into competitive jousts with the rest of humanity that are deadly serious: "To be outshone by another is to be attacked at some basic level of organismic durability. To lose, to be second rate, to fail to keep up with the best and the highest sends a message to the nerve center of the organism's anxiety: 'I am overshadowed, inadequate; hence I do not qualify for continued durability, for life, for eternity, hence I will die'" (11-12).

This vulnerability, he argues, is also what makes the pursuit of gold so universally compelling: "The thing that connects money with the domain of the sacred is its *power*. . . . It abolishes one's likeness to others" (81). Competition and gold, then, are signs of the human need and quest for inequality and the hero's power. However dispiriting this Hobbesian scenario is, it is the unavoidable cost of our unavoidable terror of death.

Because Becker's inventory of human pretension, villainy, and despair in response to the absurdity of death is so vast and unqualified, I respond first to him and assert the possibility and value of admitting death to our consciousness, before turning to the more modulated arguments of Choron.

It is very difficult to deal with, much less refute, Becker's scintillating but largely undocumented psychological assumptions in *The Denial of Death*. As he becomes more concrete and specific in his arguments in *Escape from Evil*, however, problems with his assumptions and perspective begin to come into focus and pose substantial questions about his general thesis that people cannot tolerate the consciousness of death. Considering only the two examples of death-denying behavior, competition and the pursuit of wealth, one is struck by how selective is Becker's panorama of the human condition. Is it simply true, as Becker says, that people are everywhere crushed by the fact of losing and the awareness of being "second-rate"? Without resorting to the uplifting proverbs of English schoolchildren, may one not inquire of Becker whether instances of people drawing satisfaction from having done as well as they could are not sufficient to cast doubt on what he identifies as a consistent pattern in human behavior? Losers and also-rans have the psychic incentive to perceive the greater importance of effort in a contest over the message of a scoreboard, and this "consolation prize" can be more enduring than the trophies and illusions of the victors.

The result of competition and the "diminishment" of being surpassed by others become important only in those contests played for ultimate stakes, and which represent a quest for some kind of perfection. This does seem to be what Becker has in mind when he deals with competition among people, because he speaks in various places in his book about how people defeat themselves by trying to bring absolute purity and good-

ness into the world and about the attempt "to achieve a perfection on earth, a visible testimonial to . . . cosmic importance"
(168, 136). It is crucial to ask whether the delusions of purity or
perfection of a Robespierre or a Hitler, alluded to here as the
source of evil in the world, are in any way common to humanity in general. Becker nowhere provides evidence that this is
the case. It is also critical to note how circular his argument
has become. He introduces the fact of competition among
people in general as evidence of an inability to cope with their
mortality, but competition supports his point only in those
egregious and pathological instances where the competition
involves a neurotic quest for perfection. One may inquire
whether this fierce competition is an effect of the denial of
death or leads to that denial.

This crucial point can be seen more clearly in Becker's
description of the pursuit of unlimited acquisition as a result
of the denial of death. He is convincing when he attributes the
lure of money beyond one's needs to its power to establish
distinctions among people. In this regard he confirms the
success of John Locke and Adam Smith in holding up possessive individualism as a goad to "the rational and the industrious" to test and proclaim their superiority. Becker is
considerably less convincing, however, in his subsequent arguments that wealth has some efficacy in relieving the dread of
death and achieving an ersatz immortality. He asserts that
"money is the human mode *par excellence* of coolly denying
animal boundness" by radiating its power even after one's
death, "giving one a semblance of immortality as he lives in
the vicarious enjoyments of his heirs that his money continues
to buy, or in the magnificence of the art works that he commis-
sioned, or in the statues of himself and the majesty of his own
mausoleum" (81-82). Becker allows that in this acquisitive
search for endurance modern man "might feel self-pity and
bitterness about the one-dimensionality of his immortality,"
but "in matters of eternity you take what you can get" (86).

What is remarkable about Becker's treatment of the quest
for immortality through money is that he takes it as seriously
as he does and does not deal with it as a pitifully empty and

pathological pretension. That he describes a stately mausoleum as "one-dimensional immortality," rather than as void in all dimensions, certainly belittles the significance of immortality and reveals what may be the central error in his thesis. Becker's uncritical description of seeking immortality through acquisitiveness derives from his conviction that it would be even more absurd to perceive the total vulnerability and ultimate futility of the human enterprise and not to try to hide from it. His attitude and perspective here, as throughout his work, rest on the assumption that the consciousness of death is intolerable.

It is possible, however, to take a very different perspective on this obsession that Becker sees as only testifying to how desperate humans are in their denial of death. Precisely because acquisitiveness is so bankrupt as a means of denying death, is it not reasonable to question whether the denial of death is a cause or an effect of acquisitiveness? In other words, are the frantic efforts at feigning permanence by a lead casket and stately mausoleum representative of the desperation of humanity in general, or of that part of humanity in materialistic cultures whose emphasis on competition and inequality creates awesome roadblocks to coming to terms with the enigma of death? Becker describes the demand for heroism and inequality in societies as a result and manifestation of each person's helplessness before the dualism of life and death. What he fails to realize is that he limits himself to confirming evidence at the very beginning of his argument when he simply presumes that the effort of all cultures to embody "the transcendence of death in some form" and to achieve symbolic immortality by "self-transcendence" was necessarily doomed to failure (4).

This assumption is so damaging to Becker's portrait of the hopelessness of a human response to death because it is precisely the social dimension of life that seems to be central to any secular attempt to affirm the value of our mortal human existence. Robert Jay Lifton argues that throughout the history of both secular and religious cultures the fear of death has been symbolized by separation, but that experiences of connection with other people can achieve the very symbolic immortality that Becker assumes no culture can deliver. At the very least Lifton reveals how Becker has neglected those human experiences that most directly challenge his assumption that death totally obliterates human effort and meaning. The difference one's sense of connection with other people makes in one's perspective on death also reinforces the argument that Becker may be seriously mistaking causes for effects. If it is true that a person needs interpersonal relationships in order to achieve a genuine sense of self-transcendence, then Becker's central thesis that the necessity of the denial of death causes widespread inequality, unfreedom, and social catastrophe might properly be stood on its head. We might conclude with the same data Becker cites that the inequality and social insecurity he portrays in highly competitive societies lead to, rather than stem from, the denial of death. In order to support acquisitiveness without regard to need, competitive societies must avoid at all costs the critical senses of proportion and of limits that the confrontation with human mortality provokes.

To turn to Jacques Choron's arguments against the possibility of reconciling human significance and death is not really to leave Ernest Becker's arguments, for they both see the meaning of life as undone by the impermanence of all human endeavors. Just as Becker's central flaw stems from his unquestioned assumptions about the solipsistic character of the quest for meaning, Choron's central flaw lies in the assumption that endurance is necessary for one's acts to have meaning. It is surprising how vigorously and expansively Choron applies the test of permanence to attempts at meaning in the face of death without ever considering whether life may have significance quite apart from the assurance of endurance. When he argues that neither self-fulfillment, nor moral stature, nor intellectual excellence "can be the *ultimate* meaning of life as long as it is not related to something enduring but remains an end in itself and not a means to a higher end," he offers no justification either for the requirement of endurance or for the necessity of one *ultimate* meaning of life.[8]

With endurance as his prime criterion, Choron's search for

meaning is doomed from the start precisely because human beings are not enduring creatures and have no way of testing the permanence of their mark on the world. A concern for endurance in perceiving the significance of life is productive of despair, however, not only because permanence is an unattainable goal but also because it is such a smoke screen against perceiving the more viable and more important ways in which a person's life "counts for something." Equating significance with permanence pushes the perspective on an assessment of one's life beyond one's lifetime and makes one's "immortality" dependent on the opinion of others. Conversely, disowning permanence has the momentous effect of manifesting how irrelevant external appearances and opinions are and how essential for meaning in life is one's personal assessment of the quality of one's life. In seeking to conquer the time dimension that death imposes, the search for endurance negates the obvious power every person has to affect the lives of other people, to reach beyond oneself, and to have an influence on the quality of human life that is not extinguished by one's death.

To speak of finding the meaning of life in the social dimension of our existence is, of course, to suggest the same response to and to emphasize the same oversight in both Choron's and Becker's case for the inevitability of denying death. It is important to see how these preliminary considerations reveal the incomplete perspective on human life that motivates Choron's absorption with endurance. To return briefly to his examples described earlier, we perceive clearly how much difference it makes when one dares to look at life without searching for the elusive security of permanence in human affairs. The linkage emphasized above between a concern for endurance and the reliance upon an external appreciation of one's deeds is at the heart of Choron's despair of finding meaning in even the "good life." He contends: "The often-heard argument that only a life devoted to the pursuit of pleasure and of material goods is rendered meaningless by death misses the point. For even the life spent in pursuit of goodness and beauty is so affected. It is true that 'changing one's life' might make dying 'easier,' but it does not dispose of the problem of the futility of even the good life, which death proclaims." Then Choron cites for support W.W. Dixon's conclusion that "since if the valuators perish, all values, truth, goodness and the rest, go with them into ever-lasting night, no theological or metaphysical twitterings can rebut the demonstrable hollowness of life, its inherent futility" (172). Choron and Dixon are content to draw the obvious con-clusion that the endurance of deeds and values as achieve-ments of a particular individual is dependent upon the endurance of mortal "valuators," but they never question, in the first place, why a person needs such immortality as a *particular individual* in order to have the reassurance that one's life "counts for something."

Why should a person who has contributed one jot to good-ness and beauty in the world have to meet *any* test of time in order to feel that death does not simply eradicate the efforts of one's life? It is evident here how much Choron, with much similarity to Becker, is possessed by a "monument" theory of human significance. Life for them does not have significance if the result of one's acting and creating is not objectified and made permanent in order to memorialize its mortal creator. The emphasis in this assessment of human endeavor is com-pletely on the inert result of one's action, rather than the vital act of creating itself, and upon the reaction of external obser-vers—the "valuators"—rather than the satisfaction of the actor himself or herself. It seems only a matter of common sense, however, that the issue of whether a person's existence is sim-ply a mirage in a vast desert where death presides has to be weighed according to very different criteria.

Certainly the most important point to realize about a per-son's search for significance in life is that the only judgment about significance that ultimately matters is that of the indi-vidual. It is curious that both Becker and Choron recognize so keenly how each individual's identity and equanimity are threatened by death but then focus their search for signifi-cance on the attitudes *other* people have about one's life and work. The same finality and unselectivity that make death a challenge to the meaning of each person's life are also what make it necessary for each person to be the sole arbiter of meaning in his or her life. Once we realize that it is senseless to be concerned about impressing other people with the value and importance of our life, when it is we who must be convinced that death does not make our having lived fruitless and pointless, then the evaluation of our activities changes dramatically.

With the chronicling or memorializing of events seen to be irrelevant, attention can be focused on the human actions themselves and the critical fact that, for the participant, the effort behind these actions is far more significant than their success or failure. While the performance of average people in almost any activity will be ignored by Choron's chroniclers, in the eyes of the actors the performance can have great significance if it represents what, for those people and their abilities, is a real accomplishment. Surely for them the only relevant standard of success need be whether they achieved all that they were capable of achieving.

Critics may respond unappreciatively to one's "accomplishments," but it is not the critics who have to come to terms with this person's mortality and who have to find meaning in this person's life. It is only each individual's judgment that matters as to whether actions have extended or transcended that person's being, so that death—with its sweep of erosion—still does not make it a matter of inconsequence that such a person has ever lived. Facing death itself is probably much more a test of a person's most significant talents than the acclaim of any critics. As Anatole Broyard reminds us, "in the last analysis, every death is copyrighted."9

Turning to the social context of the search for meaning may help to make this abstract point more comprehensible. As mentioned in the analysis of Becker's ideas, certainly the most important way in which people can be creators and reach beyond themselves is in the effect their actions have on the lives of other people. While Choron suggests that it is in the province of a very small elite to have their deeds remembered beyond their deaths, if he had less concern for people being memorialized by others he might note the obvious fact that there is not a person who has lived who has not had an important effect on the life of another person. One of the prime lessons of death is that we are all dramatically affected, for better or worse, by the actions of others. When we consider how capriciously we die—at various ages, of various causes—we also get a glimpse of how capriciously we live and how much the actions of others affect both our life and death. The illusion of rugged individualism is undone by noting the multitude of advantages and disadvantages people have that are completely gratuitous and beyond their control. We can make critically important decisions about priorities in our lives, but we need to be modest about presuming totally to create our personal welfare and to realize that these decisions take place within the context of our social existence and themselves have a social impact.

To recognize the necessary influence we have on others' lives is to perceive the vast opportunity each person has to find meaning in life by adding to the quality of others' lives. It is important to note how different is the "immortality" that stems from one life touching another and that which Choron sees as the great and futile human quest for ego permanence. One who brings life to others does not live on in succeeding generations by being remembered as a particular individual. Rather, the effect that a person has had upon another continues in that other person to affect, in turn, still others so that the spirit or life force of a person lives on as a permanent contribution to the human community. Each of us alive today has been shaped by countless ancestors as well as by specific contemporaries.

For an appreciation of the significance of this sharing of life, the number of people one's life affects or whether this influence is perceived and remembered by others are largely irrelevant considerations. How long one lives or the number of one's relationships are unimportant compared to the quality of those relationships. The publicizing or memorializing of the effect people have had on others' lives is trivial, compared to the question of whether those people appreciate and value their power to affect others' lives and know that this expansion of life cannot be eradicated by death.

How far this perspective on life and on death diverges from Choron is most clearly seen when he considers human love in the search for a meaning of life. "Biologically speaking," he allows, "love appears indeed as the only means, if not to defeat death, at least to limit its power; and to have progeny is possibly the only meaning of life."[10] It is so obvious here how much his equation of meaning with some form of physical endurance obscures from him the simple fact that a love relationship, with all its pain and vulnerability, creates new life in the lovers, regardless of whether it issues in progeny, and this is an event that death can bring to a close but cannot eradicate.

The same lack of vision is found in Choron's final argument that we cannot find the meaning of life in such causes as "striving to eliminate suffering and injustice and preserve peace," because "although we can devote our life to 'humanity,' humanity itself is perishable" (174-75). In Robert Jay Lifton, Choron has impressive company in this observation, but the point nevertheless only serves to emphasize how pervasive is the confusion of "legacy" and "meaning."

It is true that the continuation of human life cannot be taken for granted. Some scientists and doomsday theorists assert that our planet is statistically overdue for a collision with a supernova that could put an end to all forms of life. But this threat of annihilation need not, as Choron implies, deprive of their meaning actions aimed at improving the lot of humanity; such actions confirm in the present that people can reach beyond themselves and change the world as they find it. If they have no assurance that this world will exist indefinitely, they do know that they have left a mark on the human effort to treat people as ends rather than means, and this act of self-transcendence is a fact regardless of the eventual fate of this planet. Yeager Hudson grasps this point clearly: "A finite life is a unit. When it is finished, its quality is fixed for all times. It will always be a fact that I lived, even if no one remembers this fact. I may, by appropriate effort, constitute it a fact that I lived nobly. If I do, what does it matter that I live no more and that no one remembers? What matters is that while I live, I live well. And that really does matter."[11]

Only an insistence on the primacy of outside valuators in perceiving human significance would lead one to minimize the assurance people can find in acts of genuine sharing with others that their lives "count" and have had an impact on the human effort, even if the end of that effort is never achieved.

The purpose of this critique has not been to suggest that facing death is easy. Precisely because confronting death is not easy under any circumstance and takes remarkable struggle and courage, I have argued that the foremost error in Becker and Choron is the failure to see both living and dying in the social context. Becker in particular misses the connection between the need to deny death, which he ascribes to all people, and the fact that the terrified people he describes are trapped in a competitive, atomistic existence. Becker's fateful assumption is that the fear of death leads to aggression and competition among people, and he never considers that the causal relationship may be the reverse, that the desperate death-denying behavior he describes might be altered by a sense of connection and significance to other people that can be provided by genuinely supportive relationships. Similarly, Choron's obsession with permanence as a prime criterion in finding the meaning of life shows a lack of appreciation for the richness that experiencing the mutual support of mutually vulnerable people can bring to life.

If it does nothing more, an analysis of the views of those who see the denial of death as a necessity confirms the importance of arguments about the social ramifications of the consciousness of death. We can now see that social consciousness and death consciousness are not just tangentially related but are significantly dependent upon each other. To face death honestly is to perceive not only one's vulnerability but one's identity and equality with others and one's need for connection in the broader human community. To yoke one's ego and still value the contribution one can make to enrich others' lives, which the sense of community provides, is to have the support to face death knowing that one's life has counted for something. Given the emptiness of the individualistic existence eloquently described by Becker, we might see death not as something to be denied but as a *felix culpa* in the human condition that prods people to discover the satisfaction of living in harmony with nature and their fellow mortals.

Yet this argument against the denial of death and for finding connection with humanity in general is most gravely tested today by the threat of nuclear war, which presents new and unavoidable reasons for denying death. The next chapter examines this issue.

3. The Denial of Death in the Nuclear Era

Believing what we don't believe does not exhilarate.
—Emily Dickinson

The thinker who most insightfully and eloquently describes the avenues by which culture supports a person in accepting death paradoxically also describes a scenario in which all attempts to find significance in life can be undone by expanding nuclearism. Robert Jay Lifton is one of the most respected and authoritative thinkers now analyzing attitudes about death and the ways in which various cultures deal with human mortality. Lifton describes modes of symbolic immortality by which individuals find connection beyond their biological mortality. He develops in a score of books a perspective on death and life that persuasively counters the view that death condemns secular people to the sullen grasp of absurdity. But as one of the chief chroniclers of the physical and psychological devastation of Hiroshima and the threatening holocaust of the nuclear arms race, Lifton sees the threat of death from nuclearism as endangering the sense of connection and symbolic immortality that provides reassurance and meaning for each person in the face of "plain old death."

The progression of Lifton's arguments has set him and the rest of us up for a fall. He first provides moving perspectives of hope and equanimity in the face of death, but then he demonstrates how vulnerable these perspectives are to the very existence of nuclear weapons. Although it is Lifton's hope in his recent book with Richard Falk, *Indefensible Weapons*, that this vulnerability to absurdity will move people throughout the world to reject nuclearism, we appear to be back at square one with the absurdity of death rehabilitated by the quest for weapons of ultimate destruction. In the face of such total destruction, the average citizen experiences a psychic numbness that mutes protest and silences the demand for disarmament. Since we might hope that coming to terms with death not only would be abetted by the nuclear peril but could provide the incentive and vision for eventually freeing ourselves from that peril, it is important to examine Lifton's arguments in detail. In the end, in spite of huge debts to him for innumerable insights, I will suggest that an incompleteness in his modes of symbolic immortality limits our view of how meaning perseveres in the midst of nuclear threat and of how "ordinary death" can teach us to renounce nuclear death.

More effectively than any other writer on the subject, Lifton counters Freud's famous position on death and immortality that has encouraged so many to assume that the denial of death is inevitable. Freud argued: "It is indeed impossible to imagine our own death: and whenever we attempt to do so we can perceive that we are in fact still present as spectators. Hence the psychoanalytic school could venture on the assertion that at bottom no one believes his own death, or, to put the same thing in another way, that in the unconscious every one of us is convinced of his own immortality."[1]

As opposed to Freud's rationalist rejection of all images of immortality as nothing but the denial of annihilation, Lifton cites Jung's view that death's annihilation is less significant than the enriching value and persistence of symbolism of life after death. Lifton argues that Freud too quickly dismisses the symbolic significance of the universal imagery of immortality and that Jung fails to distinguish between the symbolic truth of the imagery and the literal idea of an afterlife. Charting a third position, Lifton accepts both Freud's insistence on confronting death as the annihilation of the self and Jung's insistence on the psychological importance of mythic imagery of immortality. Lifton focuses on the symbolizing process around death and immortality "as the individual's experience of participation in some form of collective life-continuity." A sense of immortality reflects "a compelling and universal inner quest

for continuous symbolic relationship to what has gone before
and what will continue after our finite individual lives." According to Lifton, "that quest is central to the human project,
to man as cultural animal and to his creation of culture and
history. The struggle toward, or experience of, a sense of immortality is in itself neither compensatory nor 'irrational,' but
an appropriate symbolization of our biological and historical
connectedness" (17). For him, then, death does bring about
biological and psychic annihilation, but "life includes symbolic perceptions of connections that precede and outlast that
annihilation" (18).

Lifton sees this sense of immortality expressed in five general modes: the biological, the theological, the creative, the
natural, and the experiential transcendental. The biological
mode of immortality is epitomized by family continuity, living
on through one's children and their children, with images of an
unending chain of biological attachment. He describes this as
the most fundamental and universal of all modes. The mys-
tique of filial piety in Confucianism and the role of the Roman
paterfamilias, who was both family monarch and priest of the
family ancestor cult, are classic expressions of this mode. This
mode is also extended outward from the family to tribe, organization, and nation. Lifton sees the restless search for life on
other planets partially as a struggle for the extension of this
mode. An encompassing vision of biosocial immortality, he
says, "would provide each individual anticipating death with
the image: I live on in humankind" (20).

The theological or religious mode of symbolic immortality
need not rely on a literal vision of immortal soul or afterlife.
The common thread in all great religions, Lifton argues, is the
spiritual quest and realization of the hero-founder that enable
that person to confront and transcend death and to provide an
example for generations of believers to do the same: "The lives
of Buddha, Moses, Christ, and Mohammed came to encompass
various combinations of spirituality, revelation, and ultimate
ethical principles that could, for themselves and their fol-
lowers, divest death of its 'sting' of annihilation. The basic

spiritual principle, with or without a concept of afterlife or immortal soul, is the ancient mythological theme of death and rebirth. One is offered the opportunity to be reborn into a timeless realm of ultimate, death-transcending truths" (20). The key to the theological mode is a sense of spiritual power derived from "a more than natural force" that can triumph over death.

Lifton's third mode of symbolic immortality is the creative "whether through great works of art, literature, or science, or through more humble influences on people around us" (21). An example of creative immortality is Malraux's perception that the artist participates in "the continuity of artistic creation" and that "art escapes death." Also, each scientific investigator becomes part of an effort larger than himself, limitless in its past and future continuity. Lifton relates the scientific enterprise and the previous mode by observing that the great historical transition from religion to science refers to a major shift in the imagery through which large numbers of people in general experienced the continuity of human existence. "Our psychological relationship to each of these world views lies not so much in the virtues of the one or the other as in the extent to which the vitality of either gives way to a dogmatic literalism that limits feeling and suppresses imagination" (22).

At a more concrete level of human intercourse, any kind of service or care can enter into this creative mode of continuity. Lifton explains: "Physicians and psychotherapists, for instance, associate their therapeutic efforts with beneficent influences that carry forward indefinitely in the lives of patients and clients and *their* children or posterity. . . . These issues are germane to more humble everyday offerings of nurturing or even kindness in relationships of love, friendship, and at times even anonymous encounter. Indeed any form of acting upon others contains important perceptions of timeless consequences" (22).

The fourth mode of symbolic immortality is that associated with nature itself, the perception that the natural environment about us, limitless in space and time, will endure. Lifton de-

scribes the importance to the survivors of Hiroshima of the
ancient saying, "The state may collapse but the mountains and
rivers remain." He cites as other examples of this mode the
ideology of nineteenth-century European romanticism, the
American cult of the "great outdoors," and the traditional
Anglo-Saxon preoccupations with vigorously confronting the
infinite dimensions of nature and with "cultivating one's garden." Then he notes that as "our perceptions of nature
change—to include outer space, the moon, other planets—we
continue to seek in those perceptions an ultimate aspect of our
existence" (23).

Lifton describes the fifth mode of symbolized immortality,
that of experiential transcendence, as of a different order from
the others. This mode depends entirely upon a psychic state
that is so intense and all-encompassing that time and death
disappear. Associated with expanded consciousness from experiences such as mysticism, this state can also occur in song,
dance, battle, sexual love, childbirth, athletic effort, mechan-
ical flight, or in the contemplation of artistic beauty or intellectual elegance. Ecstatic transcendence is characterized by a
sense of extraordinary psychic unity, perceptual intensity, inef-
fable illumination, and insight. It overcomes the confusions
associated with the passage of time and blends all in transtem-
poral harmony.

Lifton asserts that the special state of experiential transcendence is the indicator of the other four modes of symbolic immortality—"wildly or gently, one must psychologically travel
outside oneself in order to fuel one's participation in the larger
human process"[2]

The five modes of symbolic immortality that provide a
sense of connection for people and power over extinction are
momentously threatened, in Lifton's view, by the specter of
nuclear warfare. Lifton is by no means the first to see the
undoing of human meaning and significance by the threat of
nuclear arms. Hans Morgenthau, for instance, in an essay on
"Death in the Nuclear Age" argues: "A secular age, which has

lost faith in individual immortality in another world and is aware of the impending doom of the world through which it tries to perpetuate itself here and now, is left without a remedy. Once it has become aware of its condition, it must despair. It is the saving grace of our age that it has not become aware of its condition."[3] Lifton, however, has probably commented more extensively than any other writer on the dissolution of meaning posed by the nuclear threat. In a chapter ominously titled "A Break in the Human Chain," he sees the imagery of extinction undoing the imagery of connection most obviously in its effect on the biological mode. Our sense of radical futurelessness dispels visions of living on in one's descendents. "We are in doubt about the future of *any* group—of one's family, geographical or ethnic confreres, people or nation. The image is that of human history and human culture simply terminating."[4]

Lifton believes the image of biological severance already has vast ramifications. Losing our future, we question our past. Generational relationships, especially between parent and child, are undermined as both parent and child doubt the capability of providing security. With nuclear subversion of parental authority, "the ambivalence from both sides, always present in any case, can be expected to intensify and perhaps subvert feelings of love" (68).

Concerning the nuclear impact on the theological mode, Lifton draws on experience with Hiroshima survivors and relates that the magnitude of the experience seemed to defy the religious precepts—Buddhist, Shinto, Christian—that were available to the victims. Considering fundamentalist religious revival as compensatory and escapist, he sees religion "faced with the perhaps irresolvable contradiction of promising spiritual continuity beyond individual death in an imagined world with no one (or virtually no one) among the biologically living." In this contradiction, Lifton finds the essence of the spiritual corrosion bound up with the existence of nuclear weapons. "Once more the weapons tarnish and taint; spiritually they destroy and kill, even without being used" (71).

Lifton then argues that the mode of work and works is even more affected by nuclear threat. He acknowledges that sensitive human beings have always viewed man's works as essentially ephemeral, but the new ephemeralism envisions the destruction of *everything*, the end of human culture. "What we anticipate is on the order of a reversal of the evolutionary process—a loss of our status as the only cultural animal. We sense that survivors, should they exist, will be, by accepted evolutionary criteria, no longer human" (71).

In like fashion, hopes that our lives will be immortalized in the unending and undaunted stream of life sustained by nature are also vulnerable to the bomb. Mao Tse-tung's lyricism about "nature continuing" after hydrogen bomb tests over the Bikini Islands in 1953 has proved to be unfounded. And it is doubtful that nature, even in the long run, would survive the full onslaught of nuclear war. The impact of this realization ought to be devastating: "Destroying most or all of human life is, to say the least, an extreme transgression. But to destroy nature itself in the process is a still further transgression around which we experience a quality of dread, hidden guilt, and nothingness—these emotions frequently amorphous and beyond our grasp, but on the order of ultimately deadly sin" (76).

The effect of imagery of extinction on the fifth mode, that of the experience of transcendence, is of a different order. The experience of this mode is sought in times of crisis and vulnerability as an alternative to extinction. In the shadows, however, Lifton sees the irredeemable image of the nuclear explosion as the ultimate "high state." The sense of awe and transcendent power of bomb tests suggest that, for some, the bomb represents an enticement to experience the inexperienceable. This could mean "overcoming one's imagery of extinction and radical futurelessness by means of what may be perceived as the only form of transcendence worthy of the age, that provided by the weapon itself" (77). Lifton sees this mode as both threatened and threatening, an example of how a need "created, or at least intensified, by imagery of extinction can in turn make that actual process of extinction more likely." He sums up the implications of being "meaninglessly doomed" from the various impairments to human continuity as follows:

It would be psychologically naive to dismiss these impairments as trivial or to assume that they do not affect character formation or the emerging sense of self. From early life, relationships between self and world take on a fundamental insecurity, within a context of confusion around the threat of death (including the already-mentioned merging of 'plain old death' with grotesque, absurd death). Every attitude and human tie becomes colored by a constellation of doom, which includes, in varying degrees, fear, expectation, and embrace of that fate. There is widespread resort to psychological maneuvers designed to diminish feeling, but underneath that numbing are struggles with anger and rage along with every other kind of suppressed passion. Deep confusion and absence of meaning bedevil both one's emerging self-definition and one's larger aspirations toward human connection. [78]

As compelling as Lifton's description of the impact of nuclearism is in its perceptive and sweeping explanation of disruptions in areas from art to marriage, there are holes in his description that suggest a basic flaw in his categories. First of all, it is obvious that the threat of nuclear termination of life debilitates the five modes of immortality in markedly different degrees. Certainly a sense of connection built on biological succession would be obliterated by nuclear devastation, and the very danger of such an outcome fatally impairs in the present the pursuit of significance and immortality on that basis. Similarly, Lifton is convincing in describing the vulnerability of hopes for continuation and connection based primarily on nature or on created works. One's relationship to either of these modes is only as secure as the thread of security against nuclear devastation. It is not surprising that hopes for connection through these modes would be seriously strained in a time of tense international relations and would lead to psychological dislocation and despair.

Lifton is less convincing, however, in showing the impairment of the theological and experiential transcendental modes. He discourses brilliantly on sources of the death-of-God theology and the ironic temptation of a "nuclear high," but Lifton does not succeed in showing how the threat of nuclear destruction undermines these modes. He asserts that the promise of spiritual continuity beyond individual death in an imagined world where no one remains among the biologically living contains an "irresolvable contradiction." But why are the biologically living a prerequisite for spiritual continuity, especially for those religions that have long anticipated a cataclysmic end to earthly existence? The ethereal existence they celebrate may not be attractive to Lifton or many of the rest of us, but the mode of continuity they pursue does not seem to be contradicted or even impaired by the threat of nuclear devastation. As for experiential transcendence, Lifton acknowledges that, with its stress on connection in an ecstatic moment, this mode has only been popularized by the threat of nuclearism.

Does this mean that these modes of immortality provide a refuge from the despair and absurdity associated with the threatened destruction of the world? Not necessarily, for each of these modes, as Lifton describes them, has limitations. The theological mode has the flexibility of encompassing positions that do and do not espouse an afterlife, but depends upon a sense of spiritual power derived from a "more than natural force" that can triumph over death. This mode receives its protection of meaning against the destruction of the human world from a faith in the supernatural. Unfortunately, this mode is therefore limited to those people of the requisite faith or delusion, depending on one's point of view, and is not generally available to all people, which would seem to be a requirement for a viable mode of connection in a secular age.

The experiential transcendental mode is, by its nature, transitory and affords deliverance from the sense of separation and limitation for only a brief period. It is this transitory quality that underlies the nuclear danger Lifton sees in this mode. Some people might find in a nuclear high the same attraction that some lovers see in joint suicide: to eternalize the moment and put an end to the inevitable descent that accompanies every ecstasy.

The ambiguities in Lifton's treatment of these two modes should prompt us to reconsider the adequacy of all of his modes of immortality in expressing human continuity. The five modes are useful in describing various ways in which people seek to reach beyond themselves, but they tend to compartmentalize experiences that may be essentially related to each other and may together provide the motivation and sustenance to labor to remove the causes of nuclear war, even while the threat of that war hangs ominously over our heads.

As argued in the critique of Becker and Choron, the key to a sense of human continuity in the face of both individual death and nuclear catastrophe is the opportunity every person has to contribute to the lives of others. Lifton does not ignore this opportunity, but he treats it as just one example of ways of connecting in the creative mode. More important, he appears to ignore this vital activity completely when he assesses the impairment of the creative mode by the threat of nuclear destruction. His treatment implies that personal interaction is vulnerable to Armageddon in the same ways as other creative artifacts: if the result of one's creative efforts is threatened with destruction, one's reflection in that result can be shattered and the sense of continuity and connection broken.

Lifton is not wrong in seeing human relationships as creative, but the most significant error in his whole treatment of the mode of connection is not to see how the effect we have on others' lives is related to all of the modes, particularly that of experiential transcendence. He does not appear to see that this is the most important image of human continuity, an image that is not defeated by the threat of nuclear destruction, and an image that is the central hope of bringing an end to nuclearism.

A concern for sharing life with others relates to the biological mode in its vision of a human family with indirect but real biological and psychological linkages. This same vision finds connections with nature the sustainer of all people. This vision is not theological as such and is not dependent on the supernatural, but it can be considered a spiritual quest "to confront and transcend death" and celebrate rebirth. Finally, the image of immortality afforded by the effect one has on others' lives relates importantly to the mode of experiential transcendence. The experience of sharing life seldom has the peak intensity or time-stopping oceanic feeling that Lifton attributes to this mode, yet there is clearly an empowering sense *in the present* of transcending the limits of ego and individual mortality.

The experience of creating and transcending that can come in times of close connection with other people points up the key flaw in Lifton's compartmentalized and rather one-dimensional modes of continuity. He sees the biological, theological, creative, and natural modes as providing only a linear continuity that reaches into and is dependent upon and vulnerable to the future. It is not clear why Lifton views only the mode of experiential transcendence as providing an assurance of connection without regard to the future, but this conclusion dramatically limits his perspective on the viability of some of the symbols of continuity he describes and their role in invigorating the opposition to nuclearism.

Every person alive or who has ever lived has had an impact, for better or worse, on someone else's life. Human society and culture are products of millennia of interpersonal exchange and development. Without being presumptuous about the significance of one person's impact upon another's life, an individual can know that he or she has touched another's life, and the sense of mutual joy, or awe, or expansiveness from that experience is a powerful reassurance that one's life is not simply an indifferent event in an absurd universe.

That our actions affect others is not a choice but a given. To attempt to make that impact as mutually beneficial as possible is, as Lifton acknowledges, to be creative, but the product of that creativity is not just an improvement in another person's life but an expansion and improvement in our own. It is not hubris to recognize and value how needy human beings are of each other and how much we enrich each other's lives. In experiencing this interpersonal connection and creativity, we are not dependent upon the future in order to feel that our lives are worthwhile and have made a difference in the world. Even perceiving the possibility of our world being obliterated in spite of our best efforts, the value and significance of our lives would still be affirmed.

This is not to suggest that we can ever be indifferent to the future. Obviously the modes of connection Lifton describes do extend into the future and do exist in the present. I have tried to argue that the value of life is not held hostage by the future. Nevertheless, anyone who values human connection has an enormous stake in the future and must envision the threats of nuclearism to the human future as unspeakable crimes. This commitment to the future stems from a commitment to the present and a connection to all human beings, living, dead, and as yet unborn. This attitude toward the future and toward nuclearism is still undeveloped in the populace at large, yet it poses a hopeful alternative to the dour conclusion that nuclearism condemns one's life, and everyone else's, to total absurdity.

The best evidence of the possibilities of the more helpful response to nuclearism comes in Lifton's analysis in *Indefensible Weapons*, but it comes in the chapter *after* his treatment of the impairment of the modes of connection. He earlier describes at length the frozen numbness that results from the impairment of the modes of immortality and that keeps us from protesting the mad war games and war plans of our leaders. But he also glimpses, near the end of his analysis, the burgeoning response to nuclearism that stems from the capacity to "imagine the real" and to "join with others in moving from shame and helplessness to responsibility" (120). Lifton's analysis of the possibilities of anti-nuclearism is made with striking insights and perception. Only the origins of that movement are somewhat unclear for him, but those origins, I believe, lie in the embers of the modes of symbolic immortality that have more life than he realizes.

This discussion has begun the exploration of ways to come to grips with our mortality, but its focus so far has been on refuting arguments that the denial of death is either natural or necessary. Only when this denial is seen as not inevitable is there any point in exploring the possible political results of a greater acceptance of mortality. But it is one thing to reject the necessity of the denial of death and quite another to find ways actually to accept, and even affirm, what seems to so many an absurd flaw in the human condition. The question now becomes how can all people, whether religious or not, accept death and contradict the portrait of life as absurd?

4. Accepting Death
The Benefits of Human Vulnerability

> The dark background which death supplies brings out
> the tender colors of life in all their fullness.
> —Santayana

Writings about "accepting death" are often religious tracts or
pieces of quiet stoicism with counsels on avoiding pain and the
absorption in life that sets one up for grief. This chapter pur-
ports to be neither. In exploring the ways that we can accept
our mortality, I shall not rely on supernatural beliefs since they
are not shared by most of humanity, nor ignore the suffering
that is a frequent companion of death, a part of every life.

We must acknowledge that it is with substantial provocation that most people flee the subject of death. A glance at any
daily newspaper reacquaints us with the floods, the accidents,
the murders, and acts of human savagery that seem to belittle
life. Accounts of human violence are the most unsettling because such violence seems to mock fairness, decency, and the
fragile concepts we rely on to perceive life as whole, depend-
able, meaningful. On the large scale of violence are the accounts of one country and another sending their bright-eyed
young men off to die for this or that cause whose shining
nobility seems to a distant reader nothing but a ploy of death's
agents. To read of a commercial airliner with over four hundred peaceable people sent to the bottom of the Irish Sea to
make a terrorist's point is to feel the thinness of the line
between life and death and how death is ever ready to undo any
expectations about "normalcy" in life.

On the smaller scale, the local level, a glance at obituary

pages does nothing to lessen death's image as the capricious intruder and conveyor of anxiety, suffering, and grief. The pictures and stories give brief sketches of lives that, despite being disparate in age, status, race, and ethnic origins, all have traces of innocence and earnestness undeserving of death's rebuke and separation. We instinctively seek differences in these faces and biographies that separate them from us and our loved ones, that make their accidents or illnesses more appropriate for them than for us. But deep down, like Tolstoy's Ivan Ilyitch, we know that these stories will sooner or later touch us closely, and we will relate more personally to the plight of the relatives who place those memorial notices at the bottom of the obituary page—melancholy poems, plaintive, turgid, and unconsoling.

Our only recourse sometimes seems to be in playing the percentages—we can put off worrying about death until old age, because the really scary things that we read about in the newspapers happen only to a few unfortunate people. Chances are our lives will be perfectly normal and, for a long time, unperturbed by death's icy hand. But the quickened heartbeat at a midnight telephone ring shatters our reliance on the percentages. And try as we may to separate ourselves and our families from those unfortunate people to whom dreadful things happen, try as we may to find differences between us and them that could keep us from identifying with them and could assure us that suffering and early death are somehow more appropriate in *their* cases, we can't quite pull it off. For how can we not identify with the victim of the drunk driver, or the child who has disappeared, or the vibrant, "normal" person in whom cancer cells suddenly start multiplying? The patients in the children's hospital have personalities and potentials and agonies that are universal; they could be anybody's children. And if these awful things don't happen to us— if a child that is the light of our lives is not snatched away—we yet live with the knowledge that these things *could* happen, and thus we live with the knowledge of how exposed we are.

With this reminder of the formidable challenge before us in coming to terms with death and human vulnerability in general, let us consider how people can approach an acceptance of their mortality. In the process of making the point that humanity is not locked into a death-denying posture, either by human nature or the awesome threat of nuclearism, we have considered ways in which people could affirm life in spite of death and are sometimes aided by the reality of death. In enlarging upon those earlier arguments, I challenge religious assertions that death can be tolerated only as a gateway to an afterlife, and I seek to make the affirmation of mortal life stand on its own feet. Nevertheless, I also argue that these perspectives on death are not anti-religious and are compatible with many theological positions that do not simply use the fear of death as a trump card.

In trying to come to terms with our mortality, we might first consider that our species could not survive without death. As humanity is accustomed to taking its obvious blessings for granted, perhaps it also takes its seeming curses for granted and misses the paradox of how much death contributes to life. One important way of accommodating ourselves to the fact of death is to imagine the fulfillment of our fantasy of immunity to death. If we were not to become quickly enmeshed in a staggering population explosion and a static gerontocracy we would have to fantasize as well about an end to aging and to reproduction. With no reproduction, we would have no genetic change or renewal and, thus, would have to be satisfied with humanity's current level of development and an end to the dynamism in nature that spurs civilizational change. Would avoiding the vulnerability, suffering, and grief surrounding death be worth the cost of losing the challenge and joy of creating new life and experiencing growth in ourselves and others?

Talcott Parsons, Renee Fox, and Victor Lidy argue that death is an "important mechanism enhancing the adaptive flexibility of the species through the sacrifice of individuals; i.e., it makes certain that the bearers of newly emergent genetic patterns will rapidly succeed the bearers of older ones." Death is critically important, they continue, for supporting genetic change: "We may regard death as a major contributor to the evolutionary enhancement of life, and thereby it becomes a significant part of the aggregate 'gift of life' that all particular lives should end in death. That is why it cannot be a rational pursuit of modern medicine to try to end or even minimize the inevitable aspect of death."[1]

Psychiatrist Jordan M. Scher argues that "death provides a liberation of life stuff, permitting the renaissance and rejuvenation of the race." He finds that the phrase "The king is dead, long live the king" is an "ancient formula to represent rebirth through death." John Donne's famous admonition "Do not ask for whom the bell tolls, it tolls for thee" means, according to Scher, "not simply that a part of you has died in the dying of others, but more importantly that a part has come into life or greater life through death." Similarly, Leon R. Kass, physician and professor of bioethics, points out that "mortality, like taxation, is both certain *and indispensable* for the common good, and the common good is, needless to say, a good from which each individual benefits." Another physician, Robert S. Morison, supports this observation by noting that "if Ponce de Leon and his colleagues had ever found the Fountain of Eternal Youth, it would have soon shown itself a pool of stagnation." To rage with Dylan Thomas at the injustice of death, Morison argues, "is to rage at the very process which made one a human being in the first place."[2]

It is obvious, however, that the benefit of death for society or for the progress of civilization is hardly adequate to convince the individual who awakens at night with a premonition of nothingness that the fact of death can not only be acknowledged without illusions but even affirmed. After all, it is commonly asserted that plagues and wars and natural disasters serve a positive function for the survival and renewal of the species, but individuals experience these "helpful" events only as bitter catastrophes. The key to the individual's acceptance of death is a series of new perspectives on mortality. These new perspectives would emphasize the importance of death to a person's life in promoting honesty, a release from egoism, and an appreciation of the value of limits.

Just as society could not survive without death, the same paradox applies to the individual. We are so accustomed to lamenting and disdaining our curse of mortality that we seldom stop to imagine what our existence would be like, were we granted our unreflective wish never to die. We are instinctively enthralled by the idea of life without death, for we would be spared grief and anxiety at the loss of loved ones and the annihilation of creative endeavors. We seek surcease from the intimation of extinction, of passing from this world like an illusion, of its making no difference eventually to anyone that we ever lived. As Ernest Becker has described it, we seek relief from the terrifying dualism of being intelligent, emotional, productive creatures destined to obliteration. We know what we don't like about our mortality, but we seldom consider whether we might dislike immortality even more.

The very boon that the escape from death represents is also its torment, and this has a fearsome aspect of a higher order than human mortality. When we bring ourselves to think of not just escaping death but living into the eternal future, we quickly sense how alien such an existence would be. We cannot flesh out this fantasy, for it is not human, it has no shape or proportions, indeed it appears more like a nightmare of a bliss that is limitless, numbing, boring. The striking irony in comparing these two types of existence is that it is the very limitedness of our existence that makes life imaginable and precious. Death stamps our being as limited, fragile, and vulnerable, but the sense of limits that death conveys to us is what gives us a sense of proportion and a sense of priorities. Unlimited life, we may intuit, would inevitably render us callous and indifferent about both time and people. Seasons would come and go unremarked upon. The pull to take people and life in general for granted would be irresistible. If we took seriously the prospect of immortality (of the untransfigured variety at least), we would begin to see death as an appropriate part of human existence that gives it form and meaning, rather than as a cruel and absurd joke that deprives existence of all meaning. To realize that death unmistakably terminates our lives is also to realize that death frames our lives. In having only a

limited number of years and days, we are goaded to establish
priorities about what is truly important to us.

Socrates thought that the key difference between humans
and other animals is the awareness of mortality because that
awareness is an inducement to live an examined life. In his
Pensées, Pascal traces nobility in humans to the fact that "they
know that they die." Philosopher Peter Koestenbaum expresses this fact with a stark revision of Descartes's *cogito*: "I die
therefore I am." Koestenbaum sees mortality as the essential
confirmation of life and consciousness: "Understanding the
meaning of death is the beginning of all philosophical wisdom."[3]

It is true that legions of people, with powerful encouragement from a consumer-oriented society, resist the goad to set
priorities and to examine life. But it is, nevertheless, probably
an essential ingredient of an appreciation of life that one make
a firm determination as to what is important and valuable to
oneself. As Koestenbaum puts it: "Once he has recognized
death, the individual is on the way to becoming *decisive*. . . . By
remembering death, man concentrates on *essentials*" (11).

Psychiatrist Victor Frankel considers the claim that death
decreases the meaningfulness of life, and he responds:

What would our lives be like if they were not finite in time, but
infinite? If we were immortal, we could legitimately postpone every
action forever. It would be of no consequence whether or not we did a
thing now; every act might just as well be done tomorrow or the day
after or a year from now or ten years from hence. But in the face of
death as absolute finis to our future and boundary to our possibilities,
we are under the imperative of utilizing our lifetimes to the utmost,
not letting the singular opportunities—whose finite sum constitutes
the whole of life—pass by unused.[4]

Novelist John Fowles argues that one needs death as a fact of
life in order to have pleasure as well as significance in life:
"The function of death is to put tension into life; and the more
we increase the length and the security of individual existence
then the more tension we remove from it. All our pleasurable
experiences contain a faint yet terrible element of the con-

demned man's last breakfast, an echo of the intensity of feeling of the poet who knows he is going to die, of the young soldier going doomed into battle."[5]

Similarly, the philosopher Yaeger Hudson reacts to the yearning for an everlasting life with the conviction that such a life "could not possibly have any meaning or significance, for it would consist of an infinite number of meaningless moments or years or millennia." He argues that a life with no end would be no more satisfactory than a novel or play that has no end. "Death is the curtain on the play, the frame on the picture." Art that is completely continuous with its surroundings, with no frame to give it a definite, limited content, we recognize, he says, as the epitome of the trivial. "It is only finite life, life lived within a definitely limited span of years that can have significance. For in the life of a finite person there is urgency to live well, there are moments which are crucial, there is reason to act decisively and seize opportunities which will never return. In a life of limited duration every moment is precious, and there is real point in attempting to live it to the full."[6]

Hudson also calls our attention to the punishment meted out by the gods to Sisyphus of having to push a large boulder up a steep hill only to see it roll down again and having to push the stone up again and again. Hudson argues that what is most terrifying about Sisyphus's fate is that he can't die—his absurd ordeal must go on forever. The same may be said of the plight of Sartre's characters in *No Exit*.

One can find a good illustration of how realizing life's limits leads to a deeper appreciation of life in the remarkable testimony of many people with terminal illness. The late Orville Kelley toured campuses in the last year of his life while his cancer was in remission, relating how special each sunrise was to him and how much the quality of his life had deepened. He pleaded with the members of his audience to remember that they were all terminal and to avoid the entrapment of a rat race that fosters the denial of death and the illusion of unlimited time. Former U.S. Senator Paul Tsongas speaks in his moving book, *Heading Home*, about gaining a similar perspective after the discovery that he had cancer:

I notice if the sky is blue now. I see that God has given us the flowers
and the rivers and the sunshine. I realize that life is wondrous in its
natural and human dimensions.

There is a darkness as well. Every morning I know the fragility of
my health and I am aware of my mortality. Every day something hurts
somewhere, so I can never forget. There are new fears and new
hobgoblins to come to grips with.

But in truth my great worry is that I will lose my sense of values
and perspective as the nightmare of October 1983 fades from memory.
If I'm not ill for a long time, will I go back to the mindset I had before
the "hernia?"

I pray not. I want always to feel as I do now.[7]

Besides being necessary for gaining a perspective on life,
finiteness establishes each person's uniqueness and singular-
ity. Jacques Choron emphasizes that the consciousness of
death "goes hand in hand with human individualization, with
the establishment of single individualities." In his essay, "The
Origin of Death," George Wald points out that death seems to
have been a late invention in evolution and that "one can go a
long way in evolution before encountering an authentic
corpse." The one-celled organisms at the beginning of the
evolutionary chain did not die. Wald notes that it is "with the
sexual mode of reproduction that death comes upon the
scene." As sexual reproduction is a dramatic development in
evolution, in individualizing organisms and in certifying the
uniqueness of each organism in the genetic contribution to
descendants, so does the singular death of an organism certify
its uniqueness. The loss of immortality is the price paid for the
evolution from one-celled life forms into many-celled organisms that eventually evolved into the highly differentiated,
interdependent, singular organisms we know as human
beings. The death of these organisms is both a demonstration
of their biological imperfection and their uniqueness. Victor
Frankel explains this connection between imperfection and
uniqueness: "Just as death as a temporal, outward limitation
does not cancel the meaning of life but rather is the very factor
that constitutes its meaning, so the inner limits only add to the
meaning of man's life. If all men were perfect, then every

individual would be replaceable by anyone else. From the very imperfection of men follows the indispensability and inexchangeability of each individual; for each is imperfect in his own fashion. No man is universally gifted; but the bias of the individual makes for his uniqueness."[8]

It is interesting to observe that not only do death and sexuality arrive together in evolution, but they are also linked along with labor by the sweat of one's brow in the Genesis creation story. After eating the forbidden fruit of the tree of knowledge, Adam and Eve were aware of their nakedness and they and their offspring were sentenced to toil and eventual death. Whatever lessons this story teaches on the thorny theology of Original Sin, it is hard to react to the punishment meted out to Adam and Eve with unalloyed regret. The innocent gambolling in the pristine garden before the Fall may seem attractive as a vacation from our workaday world, but is it an attractive existence to be lived *ad infinitum*? Would any of us consider such an existence "paradise"? The very lack of limit and obstacle makes this existence unchallenging, routine, and finally uninteresting. Children are encouraged by pious elders to wonder at the folly of Adam and Eve at even being tempted by the fruit of the one tree denied them, but is it any wonder that our much-maligned first parents were inevitably drawn to challenge the single limit in their utopian existence?

Would any of us opt for a world permanently without sexuality and creative labor? In spite of the distress and crimes they have sometimes provoked, these forces seem too much at the center of what it is to be human to embrace an existence without them. And cannot the same be said for the third part of the punishment, for the Fall? In spite of all of our anxieties and grief, could we embrace an existence in the world without death? Before the Fall, Adam and Eve are simply not real personalities for us as immortal recipients of the endless bounty of the Garden. It is a life without limit and imperfection, rather than death, that presents us with a picture of absurdity.

Without referring directly to the Adam and Eve story, Yaeger Hudson argues that "the finality of death is a necessary condition for a genuinely meaningful life." His reminder that "the most intensely satisfying experiences are those which come as the result of effort and striving" raises the question whether Adam and Eve, before the curse of labor and death, were not deprived in spite of their reputed ecstasy. He concludes: "Human happiness, then, would seem to consist, at least in part, of episodes of striving punctuated with occasions of achievement and satisfaction. Eternal existence in a paradise which involved no striving, or even in a paradise in which striving were always guaranteed success, would necessarily very soon lose its taste and become extremely tedious. If such a paradise were of eternal duration, from which one would not even escape by death, it would be intolerable."[9]

Adam and Eve may have sinned as much from ennui as from pride and the presumption to rival the Creator. Still, there is no question that the sentence of mortality was an appropriate and powerful check on hubris. Along with provoking a sense of priorities and establishing each person's uniqueness, the third great benefit of mortality is its undoing of the pretensions of egoism and solipsism. There is good cause to rail against death if we want to celebrate not simply our uniqueness but our superiority over others, especially if we attribute whatever power and position we might have to our own abilities. For death equally limits the hopes and the schemes of both the high and the lowly. Although each person's encounter with death is singular, death stamps a broad equality over humanity and demonstrates a profound common vulnerability. This commonness dwarfs the distinctions that some seek as barriers in defense of privilege or national preference to separate them from others.

To state the matter more positively, death powerfully affirms our identity and connection with others during life, and is a prod to discover how this connection transcends death's biological separation from life and loved ones. It is here that we have the most important contribution of death and the most important reason not to deny but to affirm our mortality. In squashing our pretensions to individual wholeness and self-containment, death thrusts us back upon each other and im-

poses the realization that it is only the recognition and acceptance of human interdependence that give meaning to death
and life.

The link between confronting death and seeing through the
charade of heroic individualism is eloquently chronicled by
historian Gerda Lerner in describing how she and her late hus-
band faced his impending death from cancer. In her book, *A
Death of One's Own*, Lerner observes that the process of nursing a dying loved one taught her that "dependency is terrible
only for those who live in the illusion of self-sufficiency and
independence." For both the ill and the well, she discovered,
"dependence on others can be an act of grace, an acceptance of
our common human weakness. . . . Acceptance of help without false pride is the last gift the dying can make the living. It is
a handshake, a handhold, celebrating our mortality and our
transcendence of it through kindness."[10]

Though Lerner realizes that it may sound embarrassingly
sentimental to some, she finds new meaning in life from the
relationship of the nursing and the dying: "Once at least, in
each lifetime, we are meant to be a blessing to another. There is
nothing more to know than that. The rest is just blindly sub-
mitting and bearing whatever life dishes out to us" (133). That
this statement applies to both the caregiver and the patient
underlines how our vulnerability and incompleteness are, paradoxically, sources of our empowerment to make life richer for
another and, reciprocally, for ourselves.

What can we affirm, then, about our finiteness, regardless of
whether we accept a religious perspective on life? Death, if we
will look it in the face, demands the realization that life makes
sense only as it is shared with others. It compels us to yoke our
ego and observe our indebtedness not only to parents and
families but to eons of faceless, ordinary people who have
made it possible for us to live, whether biologically, physically,
culturally, or spiritually. If we consider our existence as part of
the life and history of a huge family, we realize that it doesn't
matter that our life will eventually be unknown to those who
come after us. Nor does it matter if our life is unimposing to

our contemporaries. The admonition of Scripture that one should not let the left hand know what the right is doing not only teaches against arrogance and puffery but also reassures that acts done on behalf of others are, in themselves, justifications and rewards only embarrassed by acclaim. As previously argued, all that matters is that we extend ourselves and make an effort to enrich the lives of others. That act transcends our mortality and endures beyond death. The motive for sharing life with others is not the unavailability of other absorptions because of death, but rather that death provides powerful evidence of the emptiness of those absorptions and of the reality of our identity with others.

In facing death in common, we know we are all incomplete and fragile and experience a neediness that has been the basis of community throughout history. We know deep within us the anxiety and struggle each other person has to go through in coming to terms with death and affirming life. Sadly, many people shy away from this struggle and seek to resolve the tension between life and death by denying death or by victimizing others or resorting to some other illusion of power over death. But the capacity for real empathy and connection is in every person, and this capacity confirms an enormous potential in humanity for community and social conscience. We are not talking about duty here but the discovery of our real identities, and it is this discovery that makes death bearable and valuable.

The fear of death, fed by the image of the Grim Reaper callously and capriciously terminating life and mocking human strivings and attachments, is dramatically affected by appreciating our linkage to a universal family. Consider the difference it makes whether we see a void after our death or we see others taking our place. In numerous instances parents, despite the sway of death anxieties and the survival instinct, risk their lives to save their children or even children not their own. Every person who has ever lived has made the passage from the womb at great pain and often danger to the mother. We don't find it abnormal or even unusual that a parent should unhesitatingly face death for the life of a child by, for instance, entering a burning house or undergoing a perilous operation to donate a life-sustaining organ. What dissolves anxiety about death in these instances is the love the parent has for the child and the parental desire to go to any length to secure the gift of life for the child. Also, the parent knows almost instinctively that his or her life will be continued in the child.

For very few of us will the encounter with death appear so dramatically appropriate as a confirmation of life and love, but it is not far fetched to imagine that we can all view life and death as having the same characteristics of being natural and life enriching. Our mortality stamps us as vulnerable relatives who are alike in fears, hopes, creative potential, and, above all, physical and psychic neediness that has only been relieved by the combined actions of countless other needy people.

For this very reason, death is the strongest sign of human vulnerability, but it is also a very powerful reminder of our capacity to enhance life and make it more fruitful. Not a person who has ever lived, however wealthy or impoverished, could have survived for more than a day without being cared for by other people. Not a person who has ever lived, however briefly, has not had a significant impact on others' lives, for better or worse. Precisely because *all* people are mortal and all people are therefore needy, all people have the opportunity to contribute to the lives of others. Even the infant who dies at birth has already had a profound effect upon the parents' lives. With the development of purposeful action that is only potential in the infant, the effect on others' welfare is more conscious and more significant. The extent of our interdependence is only frighteningly glimpsed in our society when we see the enormous capacity for destruction of a single hotel arsonist or airplane terrorist. Less directly, the life expectancy of everyone in the world is affected by decisions on nuclear arms, industrial pollution, and nuclear power.

We may dimly perceive how much the manner in which we die is influenced by the actions of others, but modern societies in general have a blind spot when it comes to grasping how thoroughly the manner in which we *live* is dependent on the efforts and contributions of a myriad of other people. That we cultivate this illusion of independence is unfortunate for the hubris it creates in the successful and the sense of failure it forces on the downtrodden, but the myth is even more injurious for all in masking the real creative power we have to reach beyond ourselves and to leave a permanent mark on humankind.

Here we find a most important response to those who argue that death makes an absurdity of life or that it renders life hollow and fear-ridden without the consolation of religion. The fact is that no one leaves this world without increasing or diminishing the vast web of human experience and promise. Norman Cousins summarizes this point well: "No man need fear death; he need fear only that he may die without having known his greatest power—the power of his free will to give of his life to others. If something comes to life in others because of you, then you have made an approach to immortality."[11]

This vision is not essentially utopian because no claim is made that human history is inevitably getting better. If the twentieth century teaches us anything, we can perceive that it takes enormous effort merely to keep history alive and to keep civilization and the planet from coming apart. This vision is not the preserve of an "elitist, fortunate few," as John Hick describes humanist doctrines that seek to take the sting out of death.[12] This perspective on death not only relates to the life of the poor as well as the sick but is more harmonious with the views on ancestors of tribal civilizations and family-centered societies than with those of affluent, competitive societies. The chance of a camel passing through the eye of a needle continues to reflect the chances of transcending mortality for one absorbed in possessions.

This vision of how human beings live beyond death in the lives of others is also not romantic. This view of transcending mortality does not hide from the horrible suffering that marks the life and death of so many human beings. People of all ages and descriptions are cut down, with their dreams and potential unfulfilled, by disease, natural disasters, and, more horribly, the schemes and whims of other people. No view of death can dull the pain of cancer or soften the mugger's blows or mute the screams in the madman's gas chamber. Death in all its forms is a threatening, capricious reality that routs easy formulas for success and happiness and that allows for no one a dodging of pain and suffering in this life. But neither is death the grim extermination of all meaning of life and the bleak enforcer of constant anxiety. No life is without sorrow, but one can gain a perspective on death that allows, indeed inspires, an affirmation of life.

It makes a big difference if we see death as having a necessary place in nature. It makes a big difference if we see death not as the bitter enemy of mankind but as essential to the survival of the human species. As jolted as we are by the awesome finality that death represents, if death as a limit pushes us to set priorities and consciously pursue a higher quality of life, can we renounce death? We are outraged by the randomness and capriciousness with which death arrives, and yet conception appears just as capricious; why should we disown and flail at the one end of our lives but take the appropriateness of the other for granted?

As we take a longer look at death, much of its terrifying and aggravating caprice and unfairness begin to dissipate. Some people die in ways that are horrible, painful, and inhuman, but the more fundamental fact about death is that no one escapes it. Regardless of the advantages showered so unevenly by life, no one can buy or fake his or her way out of death or out of the knowledge that he or she will eventually "walk that lonesome valley." Besides serving as the Great Equalizer and concretely demonstrating the common identity all mortals share, the universality of death also diminishes the dread of death. It is perhaps the most powerful political insight of Jean Jacques Rousseau that fair treatment is far more important to people than easy or even favorable treatment. He sees that citizens are capable of enormous labor and self-sacrifice so long as they are assured that they are not singled out for burdens. Perfect freedom and obedience are consistent for Rousseau because the law is totally depersonalized in his theoretical society; in obeying a law that applies equally to all citizens, the individual is subservient to no person and thus is free. It is a lack of fairness, rather than responsibility, commitment, or work, that is the origin of unfreedom for Rousseau.

When this insight is applied to death, the cold capriciousness and indifference of death are qualified in the realization that the ever-present threat of death and the loss of loved ones have been, and are, the fate of everyone who has ever lived. It has been fully documented by sociologists that higher rates of infant mortality and malnutrition and inadequate medical care in general relate directly to income level. The significant differences in life expectancy in this society because of income continue to be an embarrassment to our claims of fairness and equality. But though some people may be able to afford better medical care and may live to a full four score and ten, this comparative unfairness is minor in the light of the reality that all humans must die and they do not know when they will die. The very thoroughness of death's caprice should reduce our resentment and fear of being singled out by death, for *everyone* is singled out. Once we see that there are no comparative advantages or disadvantages when it comes to mortality, that death means nothing personal by its sting, then we are better able to accept death at any time as natural and as not a negation of freedom; the caprice of death is democratic in its thoroughness. This does not at all mean we should accept the caprice of other people who are agents of death, whose deeds are an outrage to freedom and justice, and who ought to be countered in every instance by the human community.

There are still two main sticking points about the fairness of death. The first has to do with the fact that some people die quietly in their sleep while others face death in terror and agony. I do not presume to dispel this troubling disparity, but I do advance considerations that might qualify this unfairness. To begin with, we might draw consolation from the arguments of some physicians that the act of dying, even violently, is not as traumatic for the dying person as observers might think. Jacques Choron reminds us of Sir Walter Raleigh cheerfully examining the sharpness of his executioner's ax and Sir Thomas More calling attention to the thickness of his neck. As for those suddenly facing accidents, Choron reports that "recent studies show that the state of mind of those facing death in accidents or natural catastrophes is characterized by a sentiment of beatitude, an unusual rapidity of thought and imagination, anesthesia to touch, absence of feeling of sadness, and finally a 'review' of past life."[13]

The obverse of this toning down of the undeserved gruesomeness of violent death is the realization that the seeming unfairness of the gentle death of those who were vicious in life is also a misperception. That Josef Stalin died quietly in his sleep or that Hitler died by his own hand hardly constitutes an escape from a life of diabolical oppression of others. It is said that both of these men were terrified for years by constant fears of assassination. Their lives fit well Plato's classic response to Thrasymachus in *The Republic* on whether the just or unjust are happier. Plato argued that the unjust live a life of constant fear, both from having made enemies and from having no reason to expect that people will treat them any differently than they are prepared to treat others. The gentle death of a person like Stalin should caution us against seeing the circumstances of one's death as a commentary either on the quality of one's life or the unfairness of death. The seemingly gentle deaths of the oppressors are hardly a vindication of their deeds, any more than a violent end for the just is a repudiation of their lives. Death is terrifying under any circumstances if the goal of one's life is to take more and more, but death is not frightening under any circumstances if one can affirm the quality of one's life.

Our way of dying *is* appropriate to our way of living in the sense that our life is a preparation for accepting or denying death. Those persons who attempt to treat life as a gift, an opportunity to share life with others, have the basic assurance that their lives are fruitful and consequential. They have the additional assurance that the circumstances of their deaths will not be a rebuke to their lives, or a source of abject distress and grief for family and friends, because the circumstances of death will be seen as irrelevant. Pain and suffering cannot negate the life-giving power each person has or the fact that one's life rather than one's death is a person's true legacy. As survivors, we do grieve more when the cause of a death can be laid to human device or human indifference than when it is brought on by nature, but our grief is for ourselves and for our society, whose flaws are manifested by such acts of inhumanity and injustice. We are galled by deaths by other-than-natural causes because they seem unnecessary, outrageously exploitative, wasteful, and untimely. Yet it is presumptuous as well as unavailing to declare any person's death untimely. For survivors, death is never timely; it comes often too soon and sometimes too late. Each life has its particular contours and dimensions, its good and bad fortune, its successes and failures, and it is not for others, even loved ones, to declare what joys or sorrows death has preempted or to demand that a life be more full than death allows. Such a demand wrongfully focuses on the death rather than the life of the person and neglects the prime importance of the quality rather than quantity of life.

This consideration necessarily leads to the other sticking point about the fairness of death: the death of the young. The same perspective that applies to painful or violent death applies to the extraordinary sorrow we feel when the young are taken by death. Children are supposed to bury their parents, not parents bury their children, and when the young meet death we feel the world is out of kilter and are numbed by the unfairness. But both death and life are perhaps more fair than we allow. If we examine our outrage at the experiences and potential that are cut short when the young die, we might see that it is more our expectations than the potential of the dying person that are cut short. The death of the young is a very cruel blow to families, but loved ones can endure this loss much better when they realize that the young life they mourn has fulfilled its potential, regardless of its age, simply by its impact on that family. Such an impact on other people endows any life with significance, wholeness, and beauty. If family and friends can realize, in their sense of loss, that *they* are the real objects of grief, then they need not feel that their inevitable and profound sorrow must be like death in its permanence and isolation. Gaining perspective on the death of the young is particularly difficult precisely because we have great expectations for the young and are inattentive to the remarkable effects their lives have upon us. But if the measure of achievement in any life is the sharing of life with others, a young person's life can be as full and complete as anyone's. This perspective will hardly rout the pain and terrible sense of loss we feel at the death of the young, but it can keep us from being absorbed and defeated by the apparent unfairness of death, and it can move us to celebrate that brief yet fruitful life.

Anyone who comments on these most profound human sorrows must be wary of sounding presumptuous or appearing to be a Pollyanna who finds solace at a time of immense human grief only because he or she is unaware of the depths of that sorrow. The obverse of chancing this pitfall, however, is to maintain a silence that enshrouds the pervasive denial of death and that leaves grieving people isolated and unconsoled. I have attempted here to see how we might accept death under any conditions for the freedom it gives the individual and for the changed attitudes toward life it may provoke in society. We need to change the way we support people in regard to death, and we need to reinforce a sense of their life-giving power to affect other people. If we can develop the cultural support in our society that honors the contribution each person can make to the well-being of others, we will not only die more easily but live more freely.

This chapter began as an effort to meet head-on the assumption that without the consolation of religion and an afterlife the threat of death is totally enervating and demands the widespread attempts we see at denying and masking it. In seeking to show that it is one of religion's smug illusions that "there are no atheists in foxholes" and to show that a secular perspective can find meaning, achievement, and wholeness in life despite, and perhaps because of, death, I do not mean to imply that this perspective is necessarily antagonistic to a religious world view, so a brief treatment of the relation of these views seems appropriate.

The argument that the meaning of people's lives is rendered invulnerable to death and time by their effect on others' lives does clash severely with fundamentalist religious convictions that see life on earth as only a passage to another life, before which human efforts at justice amount to merely a vain reconstruction of the Tower of Babel. In such a view, one's life in society is only a distraction from the path of individual righteousness. But the perspective on life and death I have argued for is not inconsistent with other, less rigid, religious positions. Krister Stendahl, former dean of the Divinity School at Harvard, argues that the "whole long and glorious Christian tradition of speaking about the immortality of the soul is only a period of the Judeo-Christian tradition, and that period may now be coming to an end." He observes that the "whole world that comes to us through the Bible, Old Testament and New, is not interested in the immortality of the soul." He notes that the only immortality for Abraham, Isaac, and Jacob was "in the loins," or as George Wald puts it, in the germ plasm. Stendahl cites the famous passage from Ecclesiastes, "the dust returns to earth, whence it came, and the spirit returns to God who gave it" (12:7), and he observes: "Here the spirit is not the individual's little identity spirit, but the life-giving power of God, the *ruach*, the wind which is withdrawn and so man disintegrates into dust. Dust to dust, ashes to ashes. . . . That's not much of immortality of the soul."[14]

As for the New Testament, Stendahl argues that there is no preoccupation with immortality, that the word is used only twice in the New Testament, and that the New Testament "speaks constantly about resurrection as against immortality." The question to which resurrection is the answer is not the question about what is going to happen to man when he dies: "The question is not: What is going to happen to little me? Am I to survive with my identity or not? The question is rather whether God's justice will win out" (77).

Concern for the power of Christ's resurrection, Stendahl says, was "a concern for where the world is going, not a concern for ourself" (78). This is why the "whole concern for individual identity, which is the technical meaning of immortality of the soul, is not to be found in the Good Book because its concern and its focus [are] elsewhere" (81). Stendahl finds promising that "an increasing number of men and women are less and less concerned about the immortality of the soul, especially their own" (78). The concern with the future of justice, with whether the Kingdom is a dream worth believing in, is "a sign of ethical and religious seriousness," and Stendahl concludes: "As a biblical scholar I must note how that concern is in many ways similar to the concerns of the first Christians as they prayed for the coming of God's kingdom rather than for their own immortality. . . . The concern for immortality appears much *too little*, too selfish, too preoccupied with myself or even my family, my race, my species. The question of prolonged identity somehow doesn't fit to what is really bothering us as we ask the questions of meaning and we seek the rays of hope" (31).

Stendahl is not alone in seeing the hollowness of religious solipsism that views the world, in the words of John Robinson, as "a vast transit camp, in which the Church's job is to issue tickets for heaven and pack people off to paradise."[15] There is a strong movement in much of contemporary religion that turns away from the egoistic love of God to save one's skin but toward a concern for what Norman Cousins calls a "higher immortality" of the human spirit that is "a richer and deeper concept than the more limited form of personal immortality."[16]

Stendahl blames the Platonic streak in Western religions for the absorption with individual immortality, but it is important to recall that in *The Republic* Plato insists on defending the just life against the unjust life purely in terms of happiness in this world. His treatment of the aged Cephalus at the beginning of *The Republic*—as a troubled, fearful man, despite his dabbling in philosophy and his pious confidence that he has paid off the gods with sacrifices—is a subtle but classic portrait of the vapidity of a religion that has no concern for justice.

Whatever the source of self-interested religion, it is enough for our purpose to note that this chapter's perspective on death is not necessarily in conflict with the religious spirit; in fact, the search for wholeness in our relations with others, whether it's called a search for the Kingdom or a search for justice, is an effort that can bring together people with very diverse backgrounds. Seeing the need for human connection as a way of overcoming the isolation of death ought to provoke both secular and religious people to reinterpret and revitalize traditional religious messages. For instance, Christian teaching and liturgy can be looked upon as primarily concerned with fostering a sense of community that is not defeated by death. Quite apart from the controversies about Christ's divinity, Christ is a hero because he was courageous about death and did not allow the fear of death to deter him from sharing life with everyone that he met. Christ's spirit lives on and sets an example of immortality by entering into others' lives, an example as stunning for people who do not ponder the mystery of resurrection as for those who do. In this view, the saints are those who have grasped with special fervor the importance of this sense of connection and the eucharist is the family meal in which people reaffirm and celebrate this connection. Redemption— the central Christian concept—is achieved by an act of faith in humanity, which is left to cultivate the seeds that represent the contribution of each human life.

If we accept Paul Tillich's definition of religion as the pursuit of one's ultimate concern, then coping with the certain prospect of death and finding meaning and fulfillment in the human community provide a rare basis in a pluralistic society for people with avowedly religious and nonreligious convictions to find a meeting ground of ultimate concern. Secular and religious people have profound differences on the explanation of human mortality, but they all must struggle to ensure that death does not finally mock life. The need and opportunity to unite in the pursuit of justice make particularly timely the moving observation of Abbé Pierre that "what matters today is not the difference between those who believe and those who do not believe, but the difference between those who care and those who don't."[17]

5. Death and Politics
The Clash with Capitalism

> Yes, sir, boy, the human animal is a beast that dies an' if
> he's got money he buys an' buys an' buys an' I think the
> reason he buys everything he can buy is that in the
> back of his mind he has the crazy hope that one of his
> purchases will be life everlastin'!—which it never can
> be—hear me?
> —Big Daddy, *Cat on a Hot Tin Roof*

If we can now see that there is a way of regarding mortality as
natural and necessary for life, we must inevitably ask what are
the preconditions for, and what are the potential results of the
spread of such a view in our society. We have seen that the
personal rewards of this view are a beneficial stimulus to
living freely and fully. A perspective that could so radically
change individual lives would necessarily have the potential
for a profound social and political impact.

One cannot help but feel the tension between a view of life
that recognizes and appreciates finitude and limits, finding
the meaning of existence in the giving and sharing of life, and
the view of life that is proclaimed in the dominant political
systems in the world today. The oppressive state socialism of
the Soviet Union seems devoted only to greater figures of gross
national product and greater controls over the lives of its citizens. The official treatment of death in which deceased heroes
are bundled off to the walls of the Kremlin, a famed few to be
specially embalmed and displayed to the ages, reflects a denial
of death as deep as in any culture. But because capitalism is the
economic system in our own society and the one we know best,
I shall focus here on portraying the clash of capitalist values

with the recognition and acceptance of death. Through such an examination we may realize the profundity and seriousness of the deep-rooted institutional resistance to changing ideas about death in our society. We may also glimpse the profundity and seriousness of the changes that are possible in political attitudes when attitudes toward death change.

Capitalism's absorption with material wealth as the indicator of success and its appeals to competitiveness as the norm in human relations betoken barren ground in which to plant seeds of hope about coming to terms with limits and death. But two factors mitigate the conflict between the consciousness of death and capitalism. One is the growing popular insistence in our society that no economics can justify the emotional costs of hiding from death. The other is that ours is not a pure capitalist system. Throughout our politics and economics we crimp the capitalist model to provide for human needs in ways that would have dismayed Adam Smith and do dismay many of his descendants. But at the very time that there is a movement in our culture to put an end to the denial of death, there is also an increasing effort to challenge deviations in our society from the capitalist model. It is argued that a commitment to competitive, entrepreneurial behavior and individualism is not only a formula for economic growth but for personal and spiritual growth as well.

In examining the inhospitable relation between capitalism and a willingness to face death, we should first consider the very beginning of the capitalist period and the political philosopher who has unquestionably had the greatest impact on American institutions and public philosophy, John Locke. Second, we should consider one of the most recent and forceful defenders of the spiritual and moral values of capitalism, the philosopher and theologian Michael Novak. In attempting to refute Novak's key argument that capitalist economics is more the victim than perpetrator of flaws in our present culture, I will later focus on the thoughts of Daniel Bell and Christopher Lasch, demonstrating how much and for how long the preoccupation with competing against other people challenges and is challenged by the acceptance of death as natural and beneficial.

As a brief prelude to the thought of John Locke, it is useful to consider his anxious predecessor in the seventeenth century, Thomas Hobbes. Hobbes has not had the acclaimed impact on contemporary political thinking that Locke has, but Hobbes is particularly relevant for our inquiry because he constructed in his *Leviathan* of 1649 an entire political system based on the avoidance of violent death. Hannah Arendt argues that "Hobbes is the only political philosopher in whose work death . . . plays a crucial role." So dark was Hobbes's vision of masterless people in a state of nature that he was convinced the citizens of his Leviathan would maintain their unreserved allegiance to an omnipotent sovereign in order to be sheltered from an existence that was, in his famous phrase, "solitary, poor, nasty, brutish and short."[1]

Hobbes's political theory allows extraordinary measures in response to citizens' fears of violent death, while totally ignoring their anxieties about natural death. This avoidance of natural death contributes to the theoretical and practical deficiency of Hobbes's prescriptions about the citizen's absolute obligation to obey the word of the sovereign. Having eschewed normative or moral inducements for the sole appeal to self-preservation, Hobbes cannot deal with the rebellion of dissident citizens who conclude—perhaps impressed with the realization that they face natural death anyway—that there are needs and concerns more important to them than the sovereign's protection from violent death. As thorough and scientific as Hobbes is in setting down precise definitions and calculations of fear, he chooses to consider only violent death as politically relevant and to leave the citizen to confront natural death in isolation, outside any social context. Hobbes, because of his daring to reason with ordinary citizens about what ought to be the extent and basis of their obligation to obey the sovereign, no doubt deserves his reputation as the founder of modern political science. At this crucial juncture modern political theory lost its standing as philosophy by treating death only as it is perpetrated by man and subject to control by political sanction. Plato's injunction that the purpose of philosophy is to teach men how to die had a very distant echo in 1649.

For many commentators, it is amazing that only one generation separates Hobbes's *Leviathan* and Locke's *Second Treatise of Civil Government*. But the stark contrasts that are usually made between Hobbes and Locke are greatly overdrawn. It is not clear that Locke had a significantly kinder view of the mass of people than Hobbes had. The traditional interpretation of Locke as an optimist about human nature and the rule of the law of reason in the state of nature ignores Locke's later comments, which contradict the anti-Hobbesian enthusiasm expressed in an early chapter on the state of nature:

If man in the state of nature be so free, as has been said, if he be absolute lord of his own person and possessions; equal to the greatest, and subject to nobody, why will he part with his freedom, this empire, and subject himself to the dominion and control of any other power? To which, it is obvious to answer, that though in the state of nature he hath such a right, yet the enjoyment of it is very uncertain and constantly exposed to the invasions of others. For all being kings as much as he, every man his equal, and the greater part no strict observers of equity and justice, the enjoyment of the property he has in this state is very unsafe, very insecure. This makes him willing to quit this condition, which, however free, is full of fears and continual dangers.[2]

In this passage Locke is not different from Hobbes in finding the origins of the social compact more in fear than sweet reasonableness, and the origin of that fear is the equal ability people have to threaten each other.

In addition, the powers of Locke's government are not as dramatically limited in comparison to the powers of Hobbes's sovereign as is usually assumed. Locke speaks of the right of the people to dismiss tyrannical regimes, but his right of revolution is purely *ex post facto* and legitimizes revolutions only after they have succeeded. And his acknowledgment of the panoply of powers and discretion allowed the executive on the invocation of prerogative in time of "emergency" would have been quite satisfactory to Hobbes. Locke does insist that government needs to have the electoral support of a majority, but when it is considered how few people were enfranchised at his time, it would be surprising if Hobbes's sovereign would not, with the barest prudence, have co-opted the support of a majority of a similar elite.

Thus, much of the dichotomy traditionally drawn between Hobbes and Locke is not convincing. Yet there is a major difference between the two theorists that accounts for Hobbes having been recognized only as an innovative theoretician and Locke having had so vast an impact on subsequent political events. Locke perceived clearly that Hobbes's appeal to the individual's fear of violent death was simply too minimal a basis upon which to structure the citizen's attachment and obligation to the civil society. Hobbes could not escape the contradiction of having to ask in an emergency that the citizen be prepared to lay down his life for the defense of a common-wealth he had joined solely for his self-preservation.[3] To the protection against violent death as the *raison d'être* of civil society, Locke made the momentous addition of the protection of property. This development had great significance for the relation between political theory and the subject of death, because in an age of incipient capitalism it was sufficient to shore up the social contract as the basis for understanding social relations and political obligation without correcting Hobbes's unphilosophical avoidance of natural death. It confirmed and hardened this avoidance into what would become a tradition. Even more significant was Locke's focus on the protection of property as an essential ingredient in the social contract, which had the effect of finding definite social utility in the public avoidance of the subject of death.

The social utility of avoiding death stemmed from the dynamic innovation Locke brought to the theory of property. The traditional defense of private property, as for instance by Aquinas, had emphasized the greater care that would be taken of an individual's goods than of goods held in common, but it had also called for regulations to ensure that property would be used for the common good. Locke argued that the world was given to mankind in common and that individuals appropriated private property by mixing the labor of their bodies, which was clearly their own, with nature. The expenditure of labor was the testimony of one's claim to private property. As Locke describes the origins of private appropriation in the early part of his chapter on property in the Second Treatise, he allows for three limits on how much property one can accumulate. First, there is the obvious limit that a person's possessions must be attached to him by his labor. Second, he must see that he leaves as much and as good for others. Third, he must see that nothing spoils uselessly in his possession. By the end of the chapter on property, however, all three of these limitations have broken down. The critical restriction on avoiding spoilage is overcome by the advent of money, which allows one to transform goods that might perish into durable currency. The requirement of labor is assumed away, as C.B. Macpherson puts it, by Locke's unargued acceptance of the wage relationship that allows one to claim the product of the labor of those in one's employ.[4] The requirement that one leave "enough and as good" in nature for others simply disappears, presumably on the optimistic assumption, later developed by Adam Smith, that entrepreneurs do not deprive others by increasing their holdings but only make nature more bountiful for all in subjecting it to their enlightened manipulation.

What remains by the end of Locke's treatment of property is the legitimization of the pursuit of unlimited acquisition. The size of a person's holdings is not an issue at all: "The exceeding of the bounds of his just property not lying in the largeness of his possessions, but the perishing of anything uselessly in it." Money, the guarantee against spoilage, has become the great elixir that opens up the vision of unbounded wealth. For his part, Locke merely assumes, again without the benefit of argument, that such a pursuit is humanity's great fascination. He asks, in trying to show how money liberates the initiative to accumulate:

Supposing an island, separate from all possible commerce with the rest of the world, wherein there were but a hundred families—but there were sheep, horses, and cows, with other useful animals, wholesome fruits, and land enough for corn for a hundred thousand times as many, but nothing in the island, either because of its commonness or perishableness, fit to supply the place of money—what reason could anyone have there to enlarge his possessions beyond the use of his family and a plentiful supply to its consumption, either in what their own industry produced, or they could barter for like perishable useful commodities with others?[5]

What Locke never considers is why, even after the advent of money, one would want to draw property to oneself beyond a plentiful supply for the present and a reasonable security for the future. Locke supposes that he is merely drawing on natural human desires while, in fact, he is reflecting a peculiar view of human nature.

It has been the great misfortune of our age and our country in particular that we have uncritically accepted, along with much that has been beneficial in staving off tyranny, Locke's doctrine on property and, seemingly, have remained unaware of how laden it is with assumptions about human values and aspirations. Acquisition far beyond one's needs has no rational purpose. Unlimited acquisition must derive its significance and lure from what it represents, and what it represents for Locke is the superior achievement of the new entrepreneurial class. For him, humanity divides into "the rational and industrious," whose labors make the earth abundant, and the "quarrelsome and contentious," who seek to live off the labor of others. The drive for superior accumulation stems from the drive to demonstrate superior rationality, and it is the fire of competition that moves one to labor and accumulate far beyond one's needs and that denies satisfaction or sufficiency, regardless of one's means.

The unrelenting pursuit of property to which Locke calls us rests at base, then, on unarticulated assumptions about human alienation and estrangement, such as the assumption that the purpose and challenge of life are to be found in outproducing and out-accumulating one's neighbor. Of course this assumption rests on the further assumption that distinctions in property acquisition derive from some *virtu* rather than from first occupancy. Locke does not deal with the question of how one becomes industrious when all the land in a society has been claimed by others more greedy than industrious. He consoles latecomers by merely pointing out that "there's always America."

There are at least two other premises, however, that are essential to Locke's description and defense of property and that have significant bearing on how our culture deals with death. First, his theory of property is based upon a very sinister view of nature. His doctrine came to be known as the "labor theory of value" precisely because it assumes the value of anything worth accumulating is derived from the labor people expend upon it. Locke tells us that nature is frugal indeed: "If we will rightly estimate things as they come to our use, and cast up the several expenses about them—what in them is purely owing to nature, and what to labour—we shall find that in the most of them ninety-nine hundredths are wholly to be put on the account of labour" (33).

Nature is not seen as having a primordial integrity that mankind need respect and be tutored by. Rather, nature exists to be manipulated and exploited. Equality was imposed upon primitive societies by the inevitable spoilage of goods dictated by nature. It was the great boon of money that this spoilage was avoided by more fluid trade, so the rational and industrious were freed from the yoke of equality imposed by nature and allowed to devote their superior abilities to conquering the earth.

Second, Locke's theory of property rests on a callous naiveté about the moral primacy and self-sufficiency of the individual. This leads him to focus on labor, after spoilage is no longer at issue, as the single criterion of one's claim to private property. His examples of appropriation are instructive: "Though the water running in the fountain be everyone's, yet who can doubt but that in the pitcher is his only who drew it out? His labour hath taken it out of the hands of Nature, where it was common

porary hedonism. A response to Novak is crucial to an argument that a new popular consciousness about death would lessen the defensive competitiveness of people. His claims for capitalism would, in effect, make the treatment of death merely a personal matter, for he maintains that contemporary capitalism already provides the best avenue to a communitarian and caring society. I shall look closely at Novak's arguments and later at those of two other major evaluators of contemporary capitalism and culture, Daniel Bell and Christopher Lasch. Bell's classic book on capitalist culture, *The Cultural Contradictions of Capitalism*, presents a balanced analysis of the barriers erected by our culture to the search for a personal identity. Lasch's *The Culture of Narcissism* presents a dispiriting portrait of the moral chaos in contemporary culture and seriously challenges the high expectations of Novak and others about the spiritual values of capitalism. An examination of these views will, I think, reveal that the inheritance taxes we continue to pay on our patrimony from Locke are very great.

As the single author who has taken the largest role in the recent debate on capitalism and values, Novak exhibits both the insights of thorough scholarship and the fervor of a recent convert to conservatism. In several recent books, he has championed the idea that capitalism is not devoid of spiritual values but has been a convenient *bête noire* for various social perspectives not compelling enough to compete in the free market of ideas. Novak's own essays in two books he edited, *Capitalism and Socialism* and *The Denigration of Capitalism*, present a perspective on capitalism and values in which spiritual values are taken very seriously and capitalism's contribution to these values is seen as uneven but generally positive. In his essay "Seven Theological Facets," in *Capitalism and Socialism*, Novak first acknowledges that, in the competition between socialism and capitalism, capitalism's claim to success usually ignores people's moral and spiritual needs:

Socialism has a major advantage over capitalism because its basic texts supply, explicitly and immediately, a moral vision. Whereas capitalist writings tend to limit themselves to economic man, a cunning abstraction from human life useful for economic considerations, socialist writings, by and large, tend to be holistic and to assume the form of moral philosophy. From the beginning, socialists have described a moral vision, and tried to imagine a society within which certain moral values are preserved. That is an important advantage.

A second advantage of socialism over capitalism lies in its stress on sociality and fraternity—an important corrective of the Anglo-Scot tradition.[6]

Novak tries hard to be fair to socialism. He speaks against the American instinct to be simplistic and reductionist about socialism and stresses the importance of thinking of socialism "rather more as a vision, emphasizing the sociality of human responsibility for the social and political order, than as a set of specific historical programs, or a mere mechanism of political allocation." Nevertheless, the great advantage he sees in the American capitalist system over socialism is that our system disperses power and influence in three different realms, whereas socialism is monistic. Borrowing from Daniel Bell, Novak argues that our system is trinitarian and composed of systems that function together: the political system, the economic system, and the cultural system. Novak sees each of these parts, while working with the others, nevertheless exercising a check and balance on the others. The key problem for socialism, he argues, is that its impulse is to collapse all three systems into one, the inevitable result of allowing the public or political sphere to determine everything.

Whatever the problem socialism has in ensuring pluralism, however, it is not at all clear that Novak's tripartite capitalist system comports with reality. Indeed, it appears that dividing our system into economics, politics, and culture is a convenient device for masking the power and influence of capitalism in all three areas and, in particular, for disassociating it from the alarming loss of values in our culture. Novak is very concerned about what he sees as the increasing reign of hedonism in our culture, but he presents a confused analysis of capitalism's role in our loss of purpose and priorities. He describes the dawning of capitalism in the Jewish-Christian culture as causing enormous dislocations that came close to destroying Western society. The introduction of a free market mechanism, he says, wreaked havoc with the ideas of community, welfare, and family by which earlier Jewish-Christian cultures had lived:

> The economic component of the system, in short, began to undercut— and to this very day continues to undercut—the other two components of the system. There are tendencies within the economic sector that generate desires, fulfill desires, and generate still more desires, so as to make plausible the notion that the pursuit of liberty is the pursuit of hedonism. These tendencies undercut the habits of discipline, saving, and restraint which make possible the accumulation of capital, wise investment for the future, and the continued health of the economic system. Thus, one part of the system can unleash forces that weaken the other two. [111]

Novak seems here to see clearly how the inducement to greed and endless desires in capitalism undermines culture, politics, and economics, but he quickly loses this clarity and begins to speak of how the culture declines independently of economics and undermines capitalism: "Reciprocally . . . the spread in the cultural sector of the system of ideas hostile to family, hostile to local communities, hostile to the kind of ascetic, disciplined interior life required for Jewish and Christian development may also undercut the political and economic systems. Because of the spread of malicious, nihilistic, and destructive ideas in the cultural sector, because of the spread of hedonism or other abuses, the disciplines required for a democratic politics become quite difficult to maintain" (111).

One looks in vain for the basis on which Novak argues that the subversion of the three sectors has been "reciprocal." He has made abundantly clear the threat capitalism poses to a culture in which community, welfare, and family are key values, but he merely assumes that other forces have independently pushed contemporary culture to nihilism and hedonism and that the culture, in turn, undermines the economic and political spheres. He sees a dire outcome in our culture from the changes that have occurred in this century, but his assumption that the three sectors are mutually dependent leaves us groping in a web of interrelated changes and unable to locate a specific cause of this deterioration. All we know is that the Jewish-Christian cultural values "modified, and were modified by, the successive economic systems in western history, and that, after having been assaulted by several generations of hostile thinkers, the cultural preconditions for the health of the economic and the political components may be undermined" (115).

The Jewish-Christian cultural values have been assaulted and perilously wounded, but this assault, rather than being hostile to the economic system, was in the service of that system and was dictated by the appeal to self-interest and greed that are at the very historical and systemic roots of capitalism. It is true that the new culture that capitalism creates also undermines capitalism, but this phenomenon points to the limits of self-interest and to a contradiction within capitalism, rather than to an unfortunate and gratuitous wounding of capitalism by the culture. If Novak were not so determined to control the damage to capitalism's reputation and to distribute the blame for our predicaments among the three sectors—"our tripartite system might be destroyed through the economic order, through the political order, or through the cultural order" (116)—he would see that if the economic sphere is not calling all the shots, it at least is the dynamo of change and clearly is faced with the results of its celebration of self-interest.

Part of the reason Novak avoids this conclusion and part of the reason he is modest in assessing the psychological costs of capitalism is that he does not see the appeal to self-interest and even to greed as all that bad. In a fascinating major section of his essay, Novak examines the ways in which he feels capitalism is not only not subversive of the Jewish-Christian values but can be affirmed by those values. Some of his arguments are truly remarkable and help to identify the alchemist's formula by which capitalism is found to be relatively innocuous, if not even beneficial, in its impact on cultural values.

Novak first argues that a Jewish-Christian culture can affirm capitalism in "its sense of experiment, openness, and innovation, which is captured by the word 'enterprise'." He sees the explosion of originality and creativity in capitalism as properly exciting the Jewish-Christian imagination: "The inventiveness of God is respected through respecting the inventiveness of human beings." If Novak seems to strain religious imagination in glimpsing it as celebrating productivity driven by profit, the second feature of capitalism that he finds attractive truly wrenches that imagination. He praises capitalist ideology for emphasizing the humbleness of the human race and the fact that we are a community of sinners. As redemption should come in the most unlikely spot, in a carpenter from a very poor and underdeveloped part of the Roman Empire, "capitalist thinkers discovered the dynamic energy to change the face of history not where it might be expected, in human nobility, grandeur, and moral consciousness, but in human self interest. . . . In the pettiest and narrowest and meanest part of human behavior lies the source of creative energy—a magnificent and, I think, absolutely Jewish and Christian insight. Where no one would choose to look the jewels are to be found" (117).

These passages demonstrate the myopic nostalgia of Novak's paean to capitalist values and the basis of his optimism and enthusiasm that capitalism not only does not lead to a spiritual void but is our only hope for seriously performing the corporal works of mercy. The key flaw in his attempt to clothe capitalism in the humility of Mary Magdalene is his comforting assurance that capitalism envisions people as a "community of sinners," though in reality the capitalist vision has no sense of community at all. Capitalist incentives are built not on the "humbleness" of human beings but on their loneliness. As we saw earlier in Locke's thought, so seminal in the development of the capitalist vision, self-interest is not a flaw in a fallen humankind, it's all that's there. People are by essence isolated, solitary atoms who survive together by observing pragmatic, self-interested rules but with absolutely no sense of identity, either as saints or sinners, and with no sense of com-

munity. It is startling to witness how as learned and sophisticated a theologian and philosopher as Novak can turn the
Judeo-Christian tradition on its head. That tradition is an
ironic one in finding virtue and magnificence in strange
places, but those places are in the hearts of the poor and the
simple, whose priorities the wealthy and the mighty are challenged to adopt, a conversion as difficult as for a camel to pass
through the eye of a needle. To read Novak, it is as though the
dynamism in this religious tradition comes from the Pharisees
rather than the poor and the humble.

Novak also calls upon us "to save the superior capitalist
sense of sin, the capitalist sense that self-interest can be re-
deemed, not by trying to repress it or deny it, but by trying to
give it expression in a system of checks and balances" (122).
These checks and balances may moderate the avarice of the
capitalists and keep them from obliging Marx's prediction
that they will be their own grave diggers, but how does capitalism redeem self-interest? The inventiveness and productivity of capitalism may well be beneficial by-products of self-
interest, but is this *redemption*, especially when that success
has only enticed us further into not a moderation but a celebration of self-interest and an absorption in competing with
other people that isolates and alienates us from them? For
Novak, the essence of capitalism is its creativity and inventiveness. The appeal to self-interest is acceptable because it is,
after all, only realistic: "Capitalism builds the sense that, in
Biblical terms, a kind of cosmic pessimism is not entirely out
of keeping with human reality." Thus for Novak capitalism is a
message of light and darkness about human nature, and he
finds it bright and dark in just the right places. Capitalism is
bright in its productivity and response to material needs and it
is dark in its realism about selfishness and sinfulness. He does
indicate some awareness of capitalism's temptation to hubris
about material success, but he is confident that capitalism is
faithful on the whole to a kind of cosmic pessimism. "The
recognition of the whole dimension of evil is implicit in capitalism, despite its often false rhetoric of optimism and progress and betterment" (118).

This last passage is very important because it seems to capture perfectly the leap of faith in capitalism that is behind all of Novak's recent plaudits for our economic system. When he highlights capitalist pessimism about human nature and rejects as an incidental mistake the rhetoric of optimism and progress, he is truly out of phase with capitalism as we know it today, and we realize that much of his appreciation of capitalism has to do with a nostalgia for the values and culture surrounding the capitalism of an earlier day. The fact is that "rhetoric about optimism and progress" is not incidental to capitalism but is its driving force. As earlier noted in the discussion of Locke's theories, capitalism creates visions of pursuing unlimited wealth and expanding power over nature and other people. It is a theory and vision incompatible with a sense of limits, a sense of priorities, and, most significantly, a sense of mortality. Capitalism approaches self-interest and hedonism with a single embrace, and Novak's attempt to drop hedonism from the arms of capitalism is as unavailing as it is confused. His failure strikingly reinforces the problem capitalism has with values in general and particularly with the need to cope with human mortality.

If we examine at length Novak's effort to protect capitalism from hedonism, we see how debilitating is this linkage with hedonism and how fanciful is the concern for values and community he attributes to capitalism. His prime argument for a split between capitalism and hedonism reassures us more about the vehemence of Novak's faith in his new-found solution to human misery than about the actual health of capitalism. He argues that capitalism could not embrace hedonism because it would be so destructive of the essential underpinnings of capitalism: "Democratic capitalism does not entail—indeed it could not survive if it were dependent upon—materialism, individualism, or laissez faire."[7] Novak presents numerous testimonies from Tocqueville to support his insistence that American capitalism does not lead to selfishness and abandonment of the virtues necessary to protect the public interest. *Toward the Future*, a letter signed by a group of conservative lay Catholics in response to criticisms by U.S.

Catholic bishops of economic disparities in the U.S. economy, a treatise that was obviously heavily influenced by Novak, quotes the following from Tocqueville:

The inhabitants of the United States almost always manage to combine their own advantage with that of their fellow citizens. . . . In the United States hardly anybody talks of the beauty of virtue; but they maintain that virtue is useful, and prove it every day. The American moralists do not profess that men ought to sacrifice themselves for their fellow-creatures *because* it is noble to make such sacrifices; but they boldly aver that such sacrifices are as necessary to him who imposes them upon himself, as to him for whose sake they are made. . . . They therefore do not deny that every man may follow his own interest; but they endeavor to prove that it is the interest of every man to be virtuous.[8]

Similarly, in *The Spirit of Democratic Capitalism* Novak makes numerous references to Benjamin Franklin in arguing that the traditional pursuit of wealth in America does not detract from communal and civic responsibilities. Novak notes Franklin's startling rejection of traditional Christian warnings against riches: "Franklin *praised* wealth and riches. He saw in them goals of moral striving. His counsel revealed a shockingly new moral attitude toward the world. The cosmos itself, the imperatives of historical progress, the call of the Creator of all things, were seen by Franklin to be impelling young men toward wealth."[9] One can agree to some extent with Franklin and Tocqueville that the American pursuit of wealth initially did not destroy a sense of community and public commitment, without agreeing with the key argument that Novak seeks to make. The point is that Novak peppers his writings with reassuring quotations from people like Franklin and Tocqueville, seemingly oblivious to the fact that most of his sources go back more than a century; this fact is crucial in understanding Novak's myopia about capitalism's problems with the human spirit. The pursuit of wealth in the times of Franklin and Tocqueville was not inevitably an avenue to hedonism and social irresponsibility because values other than greed—

what we loosely describe as the Protestant ethic—were imbedded in the culture. But these values (parsimony, humility, industry, and public service) have been steadily eroded over many decades by the self-aggrandizement championed by capitalism. It does little good now to harken back to sages whose counsels could be reassuring only to a far distant and different age.

Novak's reliance on dated texts to affirm the harmony of capitalism with values that enhance the quality of personal and community life is not accidental; he would be hard pressed to find such an affirmation in authoritative contemporary sources. The reason that Novak has to rummage among historical sources for endorsements of the benign effect of capitalism on the human spirit is that he is confused about what is central to capitalism and what is peripheral. He is wrong about the relevance to today of Tocqueville's complaisance about the symbiosis between self-interest and public interest in the same way that he is wrong in the passage quoted earlier in thinking that the "false rhetoric of optimism and progress and betterment" expressed by contemporary capitalists is incidental to the true capitalist outlook. Novak overlooks that it was the restraint encouraged by noncapitalist values in Tocqueville's day that moderated the effects of an appeal to self-interest, and he overlooks that it is the absence of such restraint today that makes the "false rhetoric" of unlimited progress truly representative of the contemporary capitalist vision.

Novak's enthusiasm about the spirit of capitalism is based both on an appreciation of earlier values that were not capitalist and are now receding under capitalism's sway and on a refusal to acknowledge how much contemporary hedonism represents the shrill, dangerous hubris of triumphant capitalist appeals. He is impressive in his concern and sense of foreboding about the reign of hedonism, but he stakes much too much confidence on denying its kinship to capitalism merely because it is destructive of the industriousness and saving upon which capitalism depends. Hedonism, however, is not destructive of capitalism's dominant appeal to self-interest. Should we be so surprised, given the evidence in Western civilization from Greek tragedy on, that a system championing self-interest would be blind to the ways in which that appeal eventually enervates and undermines that system? Novak worries about the effect of self-indulgence upon capitalism, but basking as he does in a naive, tripartite perspective on society, he assigns self-indulgence to the cultural sphere, capitalism to the economic sphere, and does not see how pervasively capitalism is driving all three spheres.

The extent of Novak's misplaced confidence that capitalism not only avoids the morass of hedonism but also contributes to public-spiritedness is seen especially in his frequent arguments in recent writings that capitalism promotes cooperation among people. He insists that critics rashly misjudge the extent of individualism in capitalist enterprises, particularly the modern corporation. Unlike the sweat shops and dark satanic mills of an earlier time, the contemporary corporation, he argues, cannot succeed without cooperation and interdependence. Novak chastises both opponents and proponents of democratic capitalism for stressing the ideology of individualism and missing the "essential communitarian character" of this system (94). He stresses how necessary it is that large corporations operate with a sense of teamwork and interdependence: "The immense literature on the problems of management today gives fascinating attention to human problems, employee relationships, and styles of personal communication. The industrial and commercial process is long and complex; a failure at any one point is a weak link in a chain. Unity of purpose is a necessary ideal. Ninety percent of a manager's problems, the textbooks say, are human problems" (132).

In seeking to emphasize the spirit of cooperation in capitalist business life, Novak seems again to confuse enlightened self-interest with actual practice. That a corporation is vulnerable to employees who guardedly, perhaps surreptitiously, pursue personal profit and self-interest, and that many employees want to pursue more long-range and fulfilling incentives, does not mean that most corporations are not thoroughly guided by the bottom line and are not prepared to forsake cohesiveness the moment it competes with profitability. It may be true that a high proportion of a chief executive officer's time "is spent in making decisions about personnel and in conveying a spirit of unity, coordination and morale throughout a farflung organization" (131), but that hardly means a corporation breeds a spirit that is "essentially communitarian." With profit as the guiding goal, the real aim for corporate students of human relations might be to create a myriad of placebo decision-sharing arrangements that do not threaten the company's central reason for existence. Corporate managers no doubt do steep themselves in textbooks on employee relations, but this may well suggest that the spirit of capitalism is wily and manipulative rather than cooperative.

To argue that enterprises would be more productive if run in a genuinely cooperative way that recognizes the legitimate rights and expertise of workers is hardly a part of capitalist doctrine. Novak's pipe dream that corporations are "essentially communitarian," merely because a cooperative spirit would be in their long-range interests, flies in the face of bedrock capitalist insistence on the prerogatives of ownership and control. Some capitalist experts on industrial relations argue against allowing even the appearance of worker participation because it leads to challenges to management prerogatives and the power of capital. In an article on "Why Motivation Theory Won't Work" in the *Harvard Business Review*, Thomas Fitzgerald, director of employee research and training for the Chevrolet Division of General Motors, points out that meaningful work reform must include the redesign of jobs and the production process with the participation of workers and with worker access to sensitive corporate information. Compare Novak's communitarian visions of the relation of labor and management under capitalism with the worries of this real-world practitioner about how even small beginnings of "cooperative relationships" would lead to serious inroads into management power:

Once competence is shown (or believed to be shown) in, say, rearrang-
ing the work area, and after participation has become a conscious,
officially-sponsored activity, participation may well want to go on to
topics of job assignment, the allocation of rewards, or even the selection of leadership. In other words, management's present monopoly—
on initiating participation, on the nomination of conferees, and the
limitation of legitimate areas of review—can itself easily become a
source of contention.[10]

One more example of Novak's unflagging optimism about
the motives of the capitalist system is seen in his enthusiasm
about the social benefits of decentralized power in our society:

The economic system of democratic capitalism depends to an extraordinary extent upon the social capacities of the human person. Its
system of inheritance respects the familial character of motivation.
Its corporate pattern reflects the necessity of shared risks and shared
rewards. Its divisions both of labor and of specialization reflect the
demands of teamwork and association. Its separated churches and
autonomous universities reflect the importance of independent moral communities. The ideology of individualism, too much stressed by
some proponents and some opponents alike, disguises the essential
communitarian character of its system.[11]

Here, as throughout his treatment of capitalism, Novak loses
sight of his antecedents. The various "its" in this paragraph
refer to "the economic system of democratic capitalism." Does
Novak seriously ascribe "separated churches" and "autonomous universities" to the capitalist economic system? Appar-
ently any attractive institutions or practices in our culture are
results of the free market economy. Any embarrassments are
chalked up to the separate realms of culture and politics that
threaten to erode the spirit and discipline of a progressive
economy.

Democratic capitalism has no special devotion to separated
churches or autonomous universities, any more than its system of inheritance reflects familial values or its specialization
of labor responds to a concern for teamwork. Family values,
teamwork, religious diversity, and free inquiry are not crea-

tures of the capitalist system and do not necessarily reflect its priorities. The needs of most families—and the principle of equal opportunity—may be far better served by greater restrictions on inheritance, just as capitalist specialization of labor can be linked to alienation and industrial anomie. It is also very doubtful that churches and universities, if capitalists had their way, would long maintain their independence from an absorption with commerce and the arts of getting and spending. Novak forgets what Milton Friedman reminds us of with ringing clarity: "There is one and only one social responsibility of business—to use its resources and engage in activities designed to increase its profits."[12]

Nevertheless, it is important that we avoid the reductionist tendency that Novak sometimes falls into and that we acknowledge that capitalism is not necessarily at war with the values he promotes. Capitalism's emphasis on efficiency and productivity has periodically provided an economic base to raise the standard of living and to allow valuable artistic and cultural pursuits to flourish. This is no meager accomplishment, but neither does it eradicate, as Novak seems to think, the underlying stigma of capitalism: that it goads individuals to heights of productivity by promoting a model of human relations that glorifies competitiveness and self-aggrandizement. It is this flaw in the appeal of capitalism that remains visible after all of Michael Novak's imaginative plastic surgery. He persuasively makes the case that there is much good in the basic instincts of the American people, but his persuasiveness ends with his assumption that most of what is attractive in our people and institutions reflects favorably on capitalism, or that most of what is unattractive is a cultural challenge to our economic system.

I have focused at length on Novak's arguments because they dramatically play down the social significance of a greater acceptance of mortality in our society. In effect, Novak is saying that such personal attitudinal changes are irrelevant to the society because capitalism already embraces the communitarian values I have emphasized in the lessons death teaches.

I hope we have seen enough problems in his arguments to glimpse the dimensions of changes in social and political attitudes that can be sparked by changed attitudes about death. The appreciation of such changes should intensify as we discuss Daniel Bell and Christopher Lasch, who point to the problems in our culture that cry out for the kind of political consciousness that facing our mortality may provide.

6. Death and Politics
The Road to Narcissism and Back

> She thought she would live forever, but forever always ends.
>
> —Linda Thompson

The analysis of Michael Novak's defense of the spirit of democratic capitalism shows that the crisis of spirit and public values that bedevils contemporary culture and that provides the context for a change in attitudes toward death has no arbitrary or accidental origin. His inability to isolate the economic and cultural realms in our society or to mitigate capitalist appeals to competition and greed with images of cooperativeness only underlines the extent to which contemporary hedonism is but a full flowering of the denial of limits in capitalist thinkers from Locke on. The treatment of capitalism and contemporary values by Daniel Bell and Christopher Lasch further supports this description of the cultural setting. Lasch more clearly connects the increasing isolation and self-absorption in our society to an inability to deal with death and aging, but this linkage is also consistent with key parts of Bell's examination of the problems and needs of our culture.

Michael Novak acknowledges that his division of society into three separate realms is inspired by Daniel Bell's thought. In *The Cultural Contradictions of Capitalism* and other works, Bell does try to make the case for the disjunction of economic and cultural developments. But this disjunction in Bell is not as firm as it becomes in Novak, and in several key places Bell allows that the disjunction is fuzzy. Moreover, Bell's arguments that appear to support Novak's defense of capitalism against the charge that it is responsible for contemporary hedonism are among his weakest. Most important, the changes Bell sees as necessary if our society is not to become totally demoralized cut deeply into Novak's confidence that capitalism is a solution rather than a problem. Bell's changes definitely require transcending the moral flaws of capitalism and, indeed, constitute a ringing endorsement of the changes that could be produced by a new acceptance of human mortality.

Bell underlines the relevance of our effort when he observes in *The Cultural Contradictions of Capitalism* that culture is centrally concerned with "how one meets death."[1] Bell's description of the interplay of economics and culture is learned, fascinating, and merits extensive summation and analysis. Basically, he disagrees with Hegelians and Marxists, who have a holistic view of society, and argues that society is not integral but disjunctive. He divides society into three distinct realms, the techno-economic structure, the polity, and the culture. Bell sees the economic order as organizing the production and the allocation of goods and services and framing the occupations and stratification systems of the society. By culture, he means expressive symbolism: those efforts in painting, poetry, and fiction, or in the religious forms of litany, liturgy, and ritual that seek to explore and express the meanings of human existence in some imaginative form. These realms have different rhythms of change; they follow different norms, which legitimate different, sometimes contrasting, types of behavior. The discordances among these realms are responsible for the contradictions within society. I focus here on the interplay Bell sees between the economic and cultural areas and on the question whether resistance to new attitudes toward death is to be expected only in the culture or in all three realms, particularly the economic area.

Bell traces the disjunction between social structure and culture in the modern period in the contrast of changing moral tempers. The culture of modernism and the economics of the bourgeois entrepreneur derive from the common thread of individualism that has run through Western civilization since the sixteenth century: "The Western ideal was the autonomous man who, in becoming self-determining, would achieve freedom. With this 'new man' there was a repudiation of institutions (the striking result of the Reformation, which installed individual conscience as the source of judgment); the opening of new geographical and social frontiers; the desire, and the growing ability, to master nature and to make of oneself what one can, and even, in discarding old roots, to remake oneself altogether. What began to count was not the past but the future (16).

This new Western view gave rise in the economic sphere to the bourgeois entrepreneur who, liberated from the ascriptive ties of the traditional world with its fixed status and limits on acquisition, remakes the economic world. The free movement of goods and money and individual economic and social mobility become the ideal, as we saw in the thought of John Locke. In the development of culture, Bell points to the rise of the independent artist, released from church and princely patron, writing and painting what pleases him rather than his sponsor. This search for independence, not only from patrons but from all conventions, finds its cultural expression in modernism. The impulse driving both the entrepreneur and the artist is a relentlessness in pursuing the new, in reworking nature, and in refashioning consciousness.

Whereas both impulses derived from the same surge of modernity, Bell argues that paradoxically "each impulse then became highly conscious of the other, feared the other, and sought to destroy it." Radical in economics, the bourgeois impulse became conservative in morals and cultural taste, and that impulse "was organized into a highly restrictive character structure whose energies were channeled into the production of goods and into a set of attitudes toward work that feared instinct, spontaneity, and vagrant impulse" (17). For its part, the cultural impulse turned into a rage against bourgeois values. Bell cites, as an example, Baudelaire who damned utility, rationalism, and materialism as barren. Baudelaire disparaged bourgeois life as devoid of both spirit and excess, showing only the "cruel implacable regularity" of industry. Bell sees culture thus driven further and further from the hold of restraint to the acceptance of impulse and to a focus on the self that becomes idolatrous. The hallmark of modernism becomes authenticity: "this concern with the authentic self makes the motive and not the action—the impact on the self, not the moral consequence—the source of ethical and aesthetic judgments" (19).

At this point, Bell seems on the verge of Novak's conclusion that the realm of culture has given rise to the selfish hedonism that abounds in modernity and has subverted the capitalist ethic; otherwise, the capitalist ethic would have maintained a blend between greed and social virtues. But Bell also provides the groundwork for rebutting Novak's conclusions, which are based on only a part of Bell's analysis of economics and culture. That part, Bell's insistence on the separateness of the two realms, is both brilliant and unsatisfactory. He allows a small elite group of artists and literati to represent the "culture" of a given period. Had he treated popular culture, the separation from the driving force of economics would be harder to show. And although Bell shows that the elite culture reacted viciously to the onslaught of bourgeois values, the fact is that it *did* react and that the economic realm set much of the agenda for the culture, even though economics was itself the target of the literati. Bell sees the economic structure reacting in turn to the challenge from the culture, but that reaction was similar only in its disdain. The economy clearly was the more forceful of these two combatants, and it clearly was the actor and culture the reactor. The economic and social structure had its own agenda—productivity, profits, power. The joust with elite culture remained an ancillary, rear guard action. Opposition to instinct, spontaneity, and impulse is not primarily an attack on the elite culture but a dictate of economic growth and capital accumulation.

Bell does not share in Novak's use of the separate realms in the society to lay blame for the loss of the work ethic at the feet of the culture. The strongest evidence for this is that Bell argues explicitly that "the Protestant ethic was undermined

not by modernism but by capitalism itself" (21). He severely
faults the culture of modernism for its idolatry of the self, but
Bell is convinced that "the breakup of the traditional bourgeois value system, in fact, was brought about by the bourgeois
economic system—by the free market, to be precise," and "this
is the source of the contradiction of capitalism in American
life" (55). Bell locates "the greatest single engine in the destruction of the Protestant ethic" in the invention of the installment
plan and instant credit. Previously one had to save in order to
buy; credit cards allow indulgence in instant gratification. The
system "was transformed by mass production and mass consumption, by the creation of new wants and new means of
gratifying those wants" (21).

Bell directly contradicts the image Novak creates of a ro-
bust, innovative, creative capitalist economy that uplifts both
the material and spiritual expectations of rich and poor alike,
and whose only impediment is the hedonism in the culture
that threatens the parsimonious and cooperative lifestyle promoted by capitalism. For Bell, capitalism itself cast away the
Protestant ethic, and capitalism's claims of creating greater
freedom are at best only partially true and certainly do not
offset capitalism's major detriment—the undermining of "ultimate meanings" in a society:

The Protestant ethic had served to limit sumptuary (though not capital) accumulation. When the Protestant ethic was sundered from
bourgeois society, only the hedonism remained, and the capitalist
system lost its transcendental ethic. There remains the argument that
capitalism serves as the basis for freedom, and for a rising standard of
living and the defeat of poverty. Yet even if these arguments were
true—for it is clear that freedom depends more upon the historical
traditions of a particular society than upon the system of capitalism
itself; and even the ability of the system to provide for economic
growth is now questioned—the lack of a transcendental tie, the sense
that a society fails to provide some set of "ultimate meanings" in its
character structure, work, and culture, becomes unsettling to a system. [21]

As vehement as Bell's indictment of capitalism's loss of
values is, however, he does not see clearly why capitalism gets

into the binds that it does. He speaks of the fateful new developments in marketing and advertising as if they are corruptions
that the economic system just stumbled into, and he does not
examine how much an appeal to competition and envy is at the
heart of the capitalist reward system. He does observe that "if
consumption represents the psychological competition for
status, then one can say that bourgeois society is the institu-
tionalization of envy." And in a footnote he exclaims with great
insight about how central envy is to an economic system that
promises unlimited acquisition: "It is surprising how little the
idea of envy has been utilized in sociological literature as the
source of status competition. A neglected writer, in this respect, is Adam Smith, who, in his *Theory of Moral Sentiments*,
declared that if people were ruled by economic motives alone,
there would be little stimulus to increase production above
necessities or needs. It is because men are driven by an impulse
for status that economic 'development' began" (22-23).

In spite of the clarity of this insight into the psychological
assumptions of capitalism and how closely it fits the portrait
of Locke's undeclared value system examined earlier, Bell exhibits confusion in much of his treatment of the moral decline
of capitalism and the role of envy and greed as qualities inher-
ing in the economic system and leading inevitably to the
abandonment of the Protestant ethic.

In analyzing the difficulty of maintaining a commitment to
the public interest under capitalism, Bell observes that "the
problem of virtue arose because of the dual, and necessarily
contradictory, role of the individual as both *citoyen* and *bourgeois*" (20). As the first, he says, the individual had obligations
to the polity of which he or she was a part; as the second, he or
she had private concerns that comported with self-interest. He
sees these motives as in conflict, but Bell does not make it
sufficiently clear that private concerns would inevitably can-
nibalize obligations to the polity in a system founded on self-
interest as a goal, and which advocates public virtue merely as
a means to that goal. Bell betrays here some of the perplexity of
his colleague Irving Kristol, who is surprised in his essay,
"When Virtue Loses All Her Loveliness," that the twin commit-

ments of the American founders to personal wealth and the public good tilted increasingly to the former in successive generations. Bell sees the role of envy in the capitalist system, but does not appear to see it as a driving, compelling, dominating role, and one is perhaps free to assume that "if only" the system hadn't come upon the device of the installment plan, or "if only" the invention of the automobile had not freed the rural majority from the local surveillance of the Protestant ethic, then capitalism might have continued the balancing act that its divines, from Locke to Smith to Kristol and Novak, ascribe to it.

This mix of stunning insight and confusion is also present in Bell's analysis of modern culture and its interplay with capitalism. This is particularly true in his brief treatment of the key issue that occasions this discussion of economics and culture, the impact on society of the acknowledgment of death and the sense of limits that inheres in mortality. With great acumen, he sees resistance to death and to limits as a crucial part of modernism and its absorption with the self. But like Ernest Becker, Bell makes the crucial mistake of assuming that it is death rather than the denial of death that leads to despair and excess: "The deepest nature of modern man, the secret of his soul as revealed by the modern metaphysic, is that he seeks to reach out beyond himself; knowing that negativity— death—is finite, he refuses to accept it. Behind the chiliasm of modern man is the megalomania of self-infinitization. In consequence, the modern hubris is the refusal to accept limits, the insistence on continually reaching out; and the modern world proposes a destiny that is always *beyond*: beyond morality, beyond tragedy, beyond culture" (49-50).

Bell cites as a colleague in this insight Saul Bellow, who, in *Mr. Sammler's Planet* reflects on the enemies of civilization: "For what it amounted to was limitless demand—insatiability, refusal of the doomed creature (death being sure and final) to go away from this world unsatisfied. A full bill of demand and complaint was therefore presented by each individual. Nonnegotiable, recognizing no scarcity in any human department" (50).

The points of Bell and Bellow are important for our purposes not only because they deal with our general topic of the
impact of death but, more particularly, because they present
the effect of death upon culture with no reference to the role of
capitalist values in this interface of death and culture. While it
is possible that they are merely taking note of how unprepared
the denizens of modern, egocentric culture are to deal with the
issue of limits, it appears that both authors could be making
the same mistake Becker does in seeing the issue of death as
threatening and negative under all circumstances and as *driving* people to impulsive excess.

The point made earlier in criticism of Becker needs to be
asserted in response to Bell's too-brief treatment of death: it is
not some innate incapacity to deal with death that pushes
people to an impulsive denial of limits; rather, it is a denial of
limits that leads to an inability to deal with death. Bell and
Bellow are correct in indicating the extreme and unfortunate
consequences of a denial of death, but their identification of
causes and effects is confused. This confusion is of course
momentous in the treatment of bourgeois economics and culture we have been pursuing, for it stems from a failure in both
Bell and Novak to realize fully how much the denial of limits
and the interpersonal alienation, which we see at full bloom in
the contemporary culture of hedonism, were endemic in the
bourgeois economic system from the start.

Bell is correct in linking the issue of death and limits to the
problems of our culture, but he is mistaken in not linking it
directly with the economic system and in not seeing by this
example how much the envy and greed promoted by the economic system have undermined the cultural realm and are
responsible not only for the demise of the Protestant ethic,
which Bell acknowledges, but also for the loss of bearings and
the aimlessness in the culture.

Such a view of the corruption of culture by the demands of
the economic realm is at odds with part of Bell's analysis and
all of Novak's. But this view gains a strong endorsement in
Bell's conclusion to *The Cultural Contradictions of Capitalism*.
This conclusion also provides as urgent an endorsement for the

impact upon culture and society as an acceptance of human
mortality may have. In his conclusion, he summarizes the
development and current state of American culture with a tone
of melancholy and alarm:

In the United States, what gave purpose to the republic at its founding
was a sense of destiny—the idea, expressed by Jefferson, that on this
virgin continent God's design would be unfolded. On a virgin continent, men could be free, prodigally so, to pursue their individual
ends and celebrate their achievements. Its doctrine was shaped by a
Protestantism which emphasized sobriety, work, and resistance to the
temptations of the flesh. . . .
    In the heyday of the imperial republic, the quiet sense of destiny
and the harsh creed of personal conduct were replaced by a virulent
"Americanism," a manifest destiny that took us overseas, and a mate-
rialist hedonism which provided the incentives to work. Today that
manifest destiny is shattered, the Americanism has worn thin, and
only the hedonism remains. It is a poor recipe for national unity and
purpose. [28]

    Bell, nevertheless, sees emerging from our loss of innocence,
assurance, and power a certain virtue: "the possibility of a self-
conscious maturity (which the stoics called the tragic sense of
life) that dispenses with charismatic leaders, ideological doctrines, and manifest destinies, and which seeks to redefine
one's self and one's liberal society on the only basis on which it
can survive." He believes this basis must be created by joining
three actions: "the reaffirmation of our past, for only if we
know the inheritance from the past can we become aware of
the obligation to our posterity; recognition of the limits of
resources and the priority of *needs*, individual and social, over
unlimited appetite and wants; and agreement upon a conception of equity which gives all persons a sense of fairness and
inclusion in the society and which promotes a situation where,
within the relevant spheres, people *become* more equal so that
they can be *treated* equally" (281-82).
    Bell gives us scant indication, let alone explanation and de-
sign, of how these three changes can be initiated and achieved.
But his vision of what is needed in our society strikingly
supports the major theme of this study. Surely we could have

no more eloquent testimony to the propensity of contemporary capitalism to blur the distinction between needs and wants and garble our priorities. Bell, like Novak, envisions society divided into the three realms of economy, culture, and polity; yet in his conclusion Bell presents a picture of crisis produced by the economy's undermining of culture, the exact opposite of Novak's description of society's present plight.

Moreover, the three conjoined changes Bell hopes for as a way out of the chaotic rule of impulse and self-interest coincide closely with the changes that we earlier suggested would result if our culture could support an acceptance of human mortality. In light of Bell's conclusion, such change is not necessarily idle speculation, for it describes a scenario of culture merely embracing its most important charge. In some ways Bell's changes describe a reassertion of culture's rightful place in helping people find significance and purpose in their individual and social lives and, as he put it at the beginning of his book, lay the groundwork for "how one meets death." This is a crucial mission on which modern Western culture has increasingly defaulted as it has alternately defied the burgeoning capitalist economy with fits of libertarianism but also accommodated that economy's dictates of continuous growth with a narcissism and hedonism that dictated in turn an escape from reality and the denial of death.

Although we have argued that culture has been more subservient to economics than Novak and, at times, Bell recognize, the core of that argument was not a deprecation of the power of culture but an insistence that capitalism's loss of a moral basis was a self-inflicted wound and not the result of attack by a secular, individualistic culture. For the three hundred years since Locke laid out the vision of unlimited acquisition for solipsistic, competitive individuals, culture has increasingly been in retreat and largely a bystander or accomplice in the spread of the competitive model of human relationships. What is different now is that capitalism is no longer the potent competitor it once was, as Bell demonstrates so articulately. The economy of growth and competition has lost the moral base that limited excess and extravagance but inspired capital investment, so the economy is now exposed to the culture of impulse it has created. As Bell points out, there is grave danger to the society in this time of economic chaos and psychological drift, but there is also the opportunity for culture to reassert itself, to challenge the empty personal identity and values capitalism has spawned, and to reassert culture's mission of providing people with a meaning for their lives with which they may confront their mortality.

Such a challenge to capitalism does not mean that the only avenue to the future is back toward Marx. The change espoused here will be most un-Marxian in that it will be pushed by a new human consciousness as people demand not so much economic liberation as a culture that recognizes and respects both life and death. The power and urgency of such a change are glimpsed in how directly an increasing acceptance of death in our culture would lead to the three changes in our society for which Bell anxiously hopes: the reaffirmation of the past; a respect for the limits of resources and the priority of needs over wants; and an agreement on a conception of equity.

We have considered how vitally an acceptance of death is accompanied by a realization that the most precious achievement we can want is to give and extend life in others, and a realization that we live because previous generations have done that for us. Realizing the finality and fragility of life is a push toward setting priorities and examining values and needs. Death manifestly challenges the illusory goal of acquiring more and more wealth and power as ends in themselves with no concern for a hierarchy of values. Finally, death is the ultimate guarantor of the democracy and equality Bell seeks. It "happeneth to them all," and death is a prod to consciousness and understanding about life and, as such, confirms not just a biological equality but a potential equality of insight as well.

In perceiving what a close match there is between the attitudinal changes that result from accepting mortality and the changes Daniel Bell finds imperative in our society, we can further appreciate the power and timeliness of putting an end to the denial of death. Why capitalist culture would encourage the denial of death is evident from the severity by which this culture is challenged by a recognition of the inheritance from the past and an acceptance of limits and of equality. The acceptance of death would seem to have a key role in re-habilitating our culture and our shared visions of a good life, as a revitalized culture has a key role in supporting a wider acceptance of death. Whereas a dated confidence in capital-ism's effect on the human spirit keeps Michael Novak from appreciating the momentousness of this reciprocal develop-ment, the lack of that confidence in Daniel Bell provokes a compelling critique of capitalism and a vigorous call for the cultural half of this reciprocal development. For a fuller appre-ciation of the importance of that cultural renewal, and for an approach to culture that sees more explicitly its connection to the treatment of death, we now examine what Christopher Lasch makes of our society's predicament and possibilities.

Even a brief consideration of Christopher Lasch's *The Culture of Narcissism* suffices to confirm how seriously mis-taken is the idea that there is nothing alarming about the effects of capitalism on the values of individuals and the cul-ture as a whole. Lasch details the terrible silence that is de-veloping when it comes to our culture's articulating for people a sense of purpose and meaning in their lives. This traditional mission of culture is subordinated to the economy's need for people to function first as economic beings and consumers in quest of new trappings of success. Like Daniel Bell, Lasch sees the economy not as the threatened victim of a confused culture but as the creator of a deep sense of drift and dislocation in the culture. Lasch also makes evident the connection of narcissism with an inability to deal with death, and thus gives some explicit indication of the significance of changed attitudes toward death in our culture. We can allow that Lasch's indict-ments do not extend to the whole of our culture, but he does describe poignantly the ominous direction in which we are heading, driven by an economic order hostile to the concept of limits and the concept of mortality.

Lasch sees as the mark of a narcissistic culture the isolation and aloneness of people in total competition with everyone else. The desperateness and absurdity of this isolated condition is masked by the applause, early on, of society and the conviction that one is pursuing "pleasure." But, Lasch insists, contemporary hedonism originates not in the pursuit of pleasure but "in a war of all against all, in which even the most intimate encounters become a form of mutual exploitation."[2] For this reason, Lasch takes issue with Richard Sennett and others who blame the contemporary malaise on the invasion of the public realm by the ideology of intimacy. In fact, Lasch asserts, both the public and private realms have disintegrated:

> The cult of intimacy originates not in the assertion of personality, but in its collapse. . . .
>
> Poets and novelists today, far from glorifying the self, chronicle its disintegration. Therapies that minister to the shattered ego convey the same message. Our society, far from fostering private life at the expense of public life, has made deep and lasting friendships, love affairs, and marriages increasingly difficult to achieve. As social life becomes more and more warlike and barbaric, personal relations, which ostensibly provide relief from these conditions, take on the character of combat. Some of the new therapies dignify this combat as "assertiveness" and "fighting fair in love and marriage." Others celebrate impermanent attachments under such formulas as "open marriage" and "open-ended commitments." Thus they intensify the disease they pretend to cure. They do this, however, not by diverting attention from social problems to personal ones, from real issues to false issues, but by obscuring the social origins of the suffering—not to be confused with complacent self-absorption—that is painfully but falsely experienced as purely personal and private. [30]

In demonstrating how the contemporary marketplace is as ruinous for individual entrepreneurs as for the culture in general, Lasch dispels the illusion of the cooperative spirit Novak dreams of in the corporate world. The narcissist has just the traits that make for success in bureaucratic institutions, which, Lasch argues, put a premium on the manipulation of interpersonal relations and discourage the formation of deep personal attachments. The management of personal impressions comes naturally to the narcissist, and he or she succeeds in political or business organizations "where performance now counts for less than 'visibility,' 'momentum,' and a winning record." With the help of Michael Maccoby's study of corporate managers, Lasch describes the key goal of the contemporary corporate manager as being "known as a winner, and his deepest fear is to be labeled a loser." As opposed to Novak's fantasy that the corporate executive's focus on personnel motivation results in visions of cooperative team work, Lasch cites a recent textbook for managers that finds success today means "not simply getting ahead" but "getting ahead of others." The new executive wants "to maintain an illusion of limitless options" and has little capacity for "personal intimacy and social commitment" (44).

Lasch sees the economic system fueling the self-interest and emptying the visions of many more than its practitioners. Advertising has become the key vehicle for shaping and reflecting national values, and he argues that advertising in the twentieth century has had a dominant impact on developing a lifestyle of narcissism. Whereas Novak plays down the power of advertising and sees important competition among advertisements, Lasch agrees with Bell that mass production "required not only the capitalistic organization of production but the organization of consumption and leisure as well." Formerly, when capitalism was still tempered by the Protestant ethic, advertising merely called attention to the product and celebrated its assets. Now, Lasch says, it also creates its own product: "the consumer, perpetually unsatisfied, restless, anxious, and bored." Advertising thus serves not so much to promote products as to promote consumption as a way of life:

It "educates" the masses into an unappeasable appetite not only for goods but for new experiences and personal fulfillment. It upholds consumption as the answer to the age-old discontents of loneliness, sickness, weariness, lack of sexual satisfaction; at the same time it creates new forms of discontent peculiar to the modern age. It plays seductively on the malaise of industrial civilization. Is your job boring and meaningless? Does it leave you with feelings of futility and fatigue? Is your life empty?

Consumption promises to fill the aching void; hence the attempt to surround commodities with an aura of romance; with allusions to exotic places and vivid experiences; and with images of female breasts from which all blessings flow.[3]

The propaganda of commodities, Lasch argues, upholds consumption as an alternative to protest. It provides an outlet by changing the more superficial areas where fashion reigns. Thus the discouraged worker, "instead of attempting to change the conditions of his work, seeks renewal in brightening his immediate surroundings with goods and services." The propaganda of consumption also turns alienation itself into a commodity. "It addresses itself to the spiritual desolation of modern life and proposes consumption as the cure. It not only promises to palliate all the old unhappiness to which flesh is heir; it creates or exacerbates new forms of unhappiness— personal insecurity, status anxiety, anxiety in parents about their ability to satisfy the needs of the young. Do you look dowdy next to your neighbors? Do you own a car inferior to theirs? Are your children as healthy? as popular? doing as well in school? Advertising institutionalizes envy and its attendant anxieties" (73).

Lasch's astute reminder of the motives and effects of advertising cuts to the quick attempts such as Novak's to sugar over the capitalist economic system and to pretend that that system does not massively affect culture and politics. Nowhere is it clearer than in the appeals of the advertising industry how much capitalism shapes the values of society, and how much the enticement to consume is at odds with people taking control of their lives and setting priorities for themselves. The only objection that needs to be raised to Lasch's treatment of capitalism is that he sees this competition and anti-social appeal of capitalism as of rather recent vintage. He draws a sharp line between the capitalism of the nineteenth century and that of today. Not only was advertising more direct and honest in simpler times, he argues, but distinction then was based on true achievement and the entrepreneur had to respond to true needs.

Lasch emphasizes the distance between Henry Ward Beech-

er, who believed that "work is more important than happiness," and the contemporary narcissists, who can only see
themselves in others' eyes and who choose celebrity over
achievement. But he deemphasizes too much the dominant
theme in capitalism that stretches from Locke through Pur-
itan entrepreneurs to the robber barons and to Madison Avenue today. That theme is the competitive pall cast over all
human relations.

When Lasch tells us that wealth is attractive only where
there is scarcity and the opportunity to compare riches, and
when he paints a portrait of contemporary narcissists vying
for a "winning image" with no concept of self but a status determined by comparison with others, we are exposed to but
variations on the same theme. The great void in the capitalist
personality, which was only partly and insufficiently filled by
the Protestant ethic, is the total absence of ends or norms in
assessing either persons or possessions. Wealth is appraised
only in comparison of one moment to another, and thus
"growth" is the key index of virtue in the capitalist catechism.
People are assessed only in comparison to other people, with
amount of economic power the essential criterion for deter-
mining worth and achievement. The aggressiveness, the envy,
the emptiness, and the despair of the narcissist are not new,
even if they now stand more naked and desperate than before.
Lasch's portrait of a significant part of our culture and population lost in the desert of narcissism is accurate and frightening,
but the winds that produced the desert have been blowing for a
far longer time than he allows.

Whatever disagreement one might have with Lasch in dat-
ing the origins of appeals to narcissism in Western culture, his
treatment of the subject is, nevertheless, particularly impressive in seeing the relation of narcissism to attitudes toward death. Like Bell, Lasch unfortunately does not give this
relationship sustained detailed treatment, but Lasch's various
and separate statements on this subject are more numerous
and precise than Bell's or perhaps those of anyone else writing
on the subject. Assembling Lasch's disparate observations on
narcissism and death, we find that these insights substantially

advance our appreciation of both the political relevance of ideas about death and the potential for cultural change in a change of those ideas.

Lasch links the narcissistic personality type with the "intense fear of old age and death" in contemporary culture and faults other social critics for ignoring this connection (33). In underlining the prevalence today of narcissistic disorders, Lasch cites the observation by Herbert Hendin that "it is no accident that at the present time the dominant events in psychoanalysis are the rediscovery of narcissism and the new emphasis on the psychological significance of death" (42). In discussing the prime strategy of corporate managers to avoid too close an identification with the company and to keep all their options open, Lasch observes: "The fear of entrapment or stagnation is closely connected in turn with the fear of aging and death. The mobility mania and the cult of 'growth' can themselves be seen, in part, as the expression of the fear of aging that has become so intense in American society. Mobility and growth assure the individual that he has not yet settled into the living death of old age" (45).

Near the end of his book, Lasch emphasizes the lack of connection narcissists feel with the past, a generational loneliness that Bell also sees as a telling flaw in contemporary hedonist culture. Lasch, however, takes this observation further and notes how this detachment from the past also cuts one off from the future and thus makes death completely terrifying. With so few inner resources, the narcissists look to others to validate their sense of self. Needing to be admired for beauty, charm, celebrity, or power, they find little to sustain them when youth passes them by. With Jonathan Schell and Robert Jay Lifton, Lasch sees abject isolation and lack of meaning in the face of death for one who "takes no interest in the future and does nothing to provide himself with the traditional consolations of old age, the most important of which is the belief that future generations will in some sense carry on his life's work" (210). The sense of isolation that Locke believed could spur entrepreneurial competition and achievement works better in enlarging gross national products than in enlarging

freedom for individual persons: "Because the older generation
no longer thinks of itself as living on in the next, of achieving a
vicarious immortality in posterity, it does not give way grace-
fully to the young. People cling to the illusion of youth until it
can no longer be maintained, at which point they must either
accept their superfluous status or sink into dull despair. Neither solution makes it easy to sustain much interest in life"
(213).

Lasch can be forgiven for not molding these powerful but
diverse ideas on narcissism and death into a general theory
about dying well and living well, for few other theorists have
even taken note of the political relevance of death and dying.
Lasch's various insights on the inability of narcissists to cope
with death emphasize not only what a prison free-wheeling,
liberated hedonists ironically come to reside in; his points also
make it stunningly clear how great a price is extracted by an
economic system that fuels its growth by promoting competitiveness among people and denying limits. Novak is as much
appalled by the aimlessness and shallowness of narcissism as
anyone, and yet Lasch shows how Novak's favored solution of
democratic capitalism is an inducement to that very com-
bative aimlessness among consumers. Lasch finds abundant
evidence that the avoidance of values by capitalism is not just a
minor imperfection we have to put up with in order to secure
the political liberty and prosperity capitalism promises. Even
if liberty and prosperity were steady and unarguable achieve-
ments of capitalism, which many would contest, these goals
quickly lose their appeal when we understand that they demand a Faustian trade-off of denying our fellowship with
others and losing our ability to cope with death.

We are not yet a society of narcissists. Millions of Americans
every day find satisfaction in aiding others and in activities—
music, art, sports, schooling—pursued for their own sake, not
merely "to get ahead." Many honest business persons and
entrepreneurs respond to creative challenges without flirting
with narcissism. But these people maintain a sense of values
and comradeship *in spite* of the manipulation of our culture by
the economic system. Both Bell and Lasch expose as mislead-

ing Novak's assumption that the capitalist economic order is being corrupted by the culture. They issue dire warnings of the spiritual desolation and psychological emptiness ahead for our population if our culture does not reassert itself against the economic system and insist on performing the central function of culture by providing meaning to people's lives and deaths.

Having seen how badly our culture needs new ideas on coping with death and why obstacles to such ideas are likely to be erected, let us examine the possible political changes a greater acceptance of death may provoke, first in regard to democracy and then in regard to the nuclear arms race. Such political changes may be fostered by the same circumstance that mitigates the supposed impracticality of proposals for the control of nuclear arms: a drastic shrinking of alternatives. Just as "realists" who hardheadedly drive the arms race toward human extinction lose all claim to that title, so also should we question claims of political realism by those whose notions of what is possible do not respond to the need of people to confront their individual mortality and affirm their lives.

7. Death and Enlivening Democracy

Death is Nature's expert advice to get plenty of life.
—Goethe

Greater candor about death is bound to affect citizens' anxieties and fears, which have always been powerful engines for political change; what, then, would be the long-range political results of changing attitudes toward death? The impact of a more open treatment of death on participatory democracy is a subject that is central and vital to visions of America's future, but one almost absent from contemporary political analysis. I will briefly portray the malaise that currently besets democratic theory, and will argue that the consciousness of mortality has its greatest political significance in bringing to life the senses of equality and community that are essential for participatory democracy. In our present culture, death and democracy are neglected, yet both challenge our passivity. No one can die for us, and no one can act as a citizen for us. As we all need to take responsibility for learning to die, we need to do the same for living. In the words of the dying poet, Ted Rosenthal, death forces the realization that "it's stage center for all of us."[1]

The twentieth century has been hard upon democratic ideals. The most effective challenge to the theory of widespread citizen participation in politics has not come from expected opponents among avowed elitists but from "realists" who have reluctantly lost faith in democratic visions. Realists argue that the democratic model must be drastically revised in the face of both complex technology and monumental citizen apathy. This theoretical revision was first clearly articulated by Joseph Schumpeter, who in 1942 redefined democracy as a process of selecting leaders rather than a vehicle of citizen enlightenment and decision making: "The democratic method is that institutional arrangement for arriving at political decisions in which individuals acquire the power to decide by means of a competitive struggle for the people's vote."[2]

The onslaught that then developed against the alleged illusion of an informed and interested citizenry has taken up an extensive portion of the political science literature over the last thirty years. To provide the context for assessing the political impact of the consciousness of death, it will be sufficient to deal only with a few highlights of the case that has been made against the "traditional" notions of democracy that emphasize popular participation.[3]

The survey research of Bernard Berelson and his colleagues showed the average voter's information about, and interest in, even presidential elections to be minimal. Berelson rescued his reader from depression over his statistics, however, by insisting that expectations about the mass of citizens had been completely unrealistic, and that the saving grace about apathy was that it allowed for a flexibility, even statesmanship, which would otherwise be restricted by a vigilant and aroused populace: "Low interest provides maneuvering room for political shifts necessary for a complex society in a period of rapid change. Compromise might be based upon sophisticated awareness of costs and returns—perhaps impossible to demand of a mass society—but it is more often induced by indifference. Some people are and should be highly interested in politics, but not everyone is or needs to be. Only the doctrinaire would deprecate the moderate indifference that facilitates compromise."[4]

Similarly, Gabriel Almond and Sidney Verba consoled the disillusioned with the observation that the myth of a scrutinizing public had utility in those times when leaders, though selected only from among competing elites, might become grossly negligent of due process and public opinion. Maintaining the illusion that the will of the people is dominant in routine matters would increase the likelihood that the public could be roused to discipline errant leaders in those exceptional times of obvious incompetence or malfeasance when the equilibrium of the system is threatened. Also, the expectation that gross indifference to the public would invite this retribution served as a check on the regular activities of elites, and this was reassuringly described by Almond and Verba as "the law of anticipated reactions."[5]

Thus the realists' rejection of the optimistic ends of traditional democratic theory tended generally to be accompanied by a contentment with democratic procedures as a way of ensuring both popular support for government and an ultimate check upon tyrannical or grossly incompetent governmental policies. The pluralist persuasion seems generally to derive an equanimity from this marginal utility of democracy, despite a loss of faith in the masses. Hence Robert Dahl's satisfaction with a model of government that allows a significant broker's role for elected political leaders and a dispersed influence of elites—an alternative to the model of a stratified society portrayed by C. Wright Mills, Floyd Hunter, and others.

There are, however, telling criticisms to be registered against these revisionists of democracy. After more than two decades and much discussion, there is still great force in the argument by Peter Bachrach and Morton Baratz that the pluralists, in spite of their rejection of traditional democratic ideals, greatly overestimate the prospects of an open political system.[6] Criticizing Dahl in particular for being satisfied with finding competition surrounding headline controversies and for not considering that many issues vital to the public welfare may never even be raised because of the influence of a privileged elite, Bachrach and Baratz force the question whether the realists' demythologizing of democracy has not given rise to a series of other myths. The apathy that Berelson and his colleagues celebrate as making for flexibility and compromise has that effect precisely because it is easier to compromise the interests of those who are uninformed and unpolitical. Similarly, Almond and Verba show little recognition of how signifi-

cantly the popular voice has been reduced by the law of anticipated reactions to an after-the-fact veto, or of how far an elite
may go in disguising its policies and protecting them from this
reaction. Having based this theory on the general public's
naiveté in not grasping the extent to which their control has
been eroded, why should Almond and Verba suddenly find
hope in the public's sophistication to penetrate the public
relations smoke screens of an offending regime?

Unfortunately for the vitality of democracy, all of these criticisms from the revisionists attack complacency without offer-
ing satisfying alternatives that lead to a politics of widespread
popular participation. The critique of the practicality and
possibility of that participation has gone almost unscathed. In
one of the earliest and most provocative indictments of the
realists' research methods, Jack Walker argued that the realists err in taking the lack of specifically political turmoil and
unrest as a sign of popular contentment with an ineffective
political role. Walker argued that indices of social unrest, such
as crime rates, would challenge this portrait of satisfied apathy. But the criticism also goes to the revisionists' smugness
about coping with apathy, not to their conviction that there is a
widespread disinclination to participate in politics. Walker's
implication is that the political system, rather than the citizen,
is at fault. But, as Dahl was quick to point out, no concrete
suggestions are made for changing the system so as to generate
greater citizen participation.[7]

Among the few imaginative attempts to formulate changes
that would increase popular participation in politics are studies by Carole Pateman, Peter Bachrach, and Benjamin Barber.
These authors argue that for democracy to be real and in order
to gain the experience necessary for active citizenship, people
must be given an opportunity to contribute to decisions that
immediately affect them and in which they have an interest
and some expertise. Barber notes that defenders of representative democracy are fond of citing failure of citizen participation where there has been no preparation and practice for
participation. "Such a course," he argues, "in truth merely

gives the people all the insignia and none of the tools of citizenship and then convicts them of incompetence."[8] The locus of participation becomes the workplace, and a strong case is made by these authors for the political and public character of much supposedly private enterprise and for the legitimacy of significant worker input. This change, nevertheless, while attractive in at least initiating participation, by itself must be limited in scope because it does not open up greater participation in the important value decisions in a society that can easily preempt local decisions made in the workplace. The U.S. Steel plant in Birmingham, Alabama, which Bachrach cites in an example, might well be steered by worker direction to having a different impact on local racial desegregation, yet decisions regarding actual production in the plant would be almost entirely dependent upon decisions made in Washington and elsewhere.

What is even more problematic about proposals for participatory democracy is that they reject without refuting the basic revisionist claim that the mass of people are simply not interested either in making these decisions or in the necessary expansion of what is defined as public, as opposed to private, business—a change that is an essential preliminary to opening up the political process. When one is reminded by Mulford Sibley of how thoroughly we have privatized such important events as technological change and with what disastrous effect upon democracy, one has a keener appreciation of the obstacles to change: "Until Americans develop the law, standards, practice, and organization for deliberate public introduction or rejection of complex technology, their supposed self-government will remain merely a pretence. As it is now, they allow Fortune and a multitude of immediate profit-motivated decisions to shape their destiny. Then within the limits of this Fate and those profit-motivated decisions, they make relatively minor choices about how they will 'adjust' to the major decisions about which they have not been consulted."[9]

Samuel Bowles and Herbert Gintis remind us that even with his firm pluralist roots Robert Dahl now "wonders pointedly why property rights should predominate over the democratic rights of workers in the modern corporation," and Benjamin Barber notes that Dahl "has begun to question the capacity of pluralism . . . to deal with questions of economic and social justice." Nevertheless, are we—and Dahl—left unable to respond to the modern enthrallment with privacy and acquisitiveness? Consider his earlier description: "Typically, as a source of direct gratifications, political activity will appear to homo civicus as less attractive than a host of other activities; and, as a strategy to achieve his gratifications indirectly political action will seem considerably less efficient than working at his job, earning more money, taking out insurance, joining a club, planning a vacation, moving to another neighborhood or city, or coping with an uncertain future in manifold other ways."[10]

It is interesting and depressing to note that the contemporary political theorist most concerned with "public happiness" that comes from appearing and speaking in the public forum, Hannah Arendt, sees this essential activity as the prize of the few while the mass of other people is exiled to the apolitical quest of wealth and accumulation. She argues that "freedom and luxury have always been thought to be incompatible," and she laments "the ravages with which American prosperity and American mass society increasingly threaten the whole political realm."[11]

Arendt's comments are a reminder that popular participation is losing its relevance not simply among the pluralist revisionists of democratic theory; among some social theorists who consider seriously the various crises that now beset governments, the prospects for democracy are even bleaker than they are for the revisionists. Robert Heilbroner, for example, is dismally convinced that meeting the challenges of nuclear expansion, overpopulation, and the decay of the environment "may be possible only under governments capable of rallying obedience far more effectively than would be possible in a democratic setting." Heilbroner envisions a postindustrial society that will have to enforce public over private priorities and

radically limit "the pleasures of political, social, and intellectual freedom" that make democracy possible and desirable.[12]

With the Scylla of public indifference on the one side of
democracy and the Charybdis of authoritarian response to
crisis on the other, the subject of death may seem relevant to
this discussion only as a diversion in the frustration of political
aspirations. This is precisely Herbert Marcuse's point when he
alleges that modern regimes promote a concern for death so
that citizens, seeking relief from their anxieties, will embrace
repressive policies. In one of the rare commentaries on death
by a contemporary political philosopher, Marcuse argues that
"the glorifying acceptance of death, which carries with it the
acceptance of the political order, also marks the birth of philosophical morality. . . . The fearful acceptance of death has
become an integral element of public and private morality."[13]
But this repressive effect of the association of death and politics is not new. The paradigm of authoritarianism in modern
political theory comes from Hobbes, who constructed his *Levi-*
athan fundamentally on the fear of violent death. Mussolini
likewise was convinced that the evidence of fascism's power
and attraction could be found in the release it provided from
the lonely fear of death: "that this faith is very powerful in the
minds of men is demonstrated by those who have suffered and
died for it." Speaking about the years that preceded the march
to Rome, Mussolini asserted "there was much discussion but—
what was more important and more sacred—men died. They
knew how to die." Mussolini and other fascists saw liberal
democracy's salient flaw in the contradiction it confronted in
death and crisis. Alfredo Rocco, one of Mussolini's chief apolo-
gists, saw the telling need and cost of the denial of death in
individualist culture in a quotation from Mazzini: "The decla-
ration of rights, which all constitutions insist on copying slav-
ishly from the French, expresses only those of the period. . . .
which considered the individual as the end and pointed out
only one half of the problem. . . . Assume the existence of one
of those crises that threaten the life of the nation, and demand
the active sacrifice of all its sons. . . . Will you ask the citizens

to face martyrdom in virtue of their rights? You have taught
men that society was solely constituted to guarantee their
rights and now you ask them to sacrifice one and all, to suffer
and die for the safety of the 'nation'?"[14]

Finally, we recall that Ernest Becker makes perhaps the
most striking and direct linking of death and authoritarianism. He alleges that people cannot tolerate the awareness of
death and that their frantic effort to deny their mortality leads
to strongly anti-democratic behavior. He argues that because
human beings cannot deal with death, they cannot deal with
freedom and are driven to seek the protection of a forceful
leader, whose power in political jousts symbolizes a power
against the great enemy, death. Competition among people
and the pursuit of money are seen by Becker as inevitable as
they are undemocratic, for they are the signs of the human
demand for inequality and the power of the hero.

These attempts from Hobbes to Becker to draw imperatives
for authoritarianism from the consciousness of death are impressive in the simplicity with which they explain a seemingly
compulsive avoidance of freedom and political participation.
Yet, as we have already seen, they all rest on rather simple and
basic oversights. Hobbes is momentously incomplete in his
treatment of death, inasmuch as he responds only to citizens'
fear of violent death and not natural death. This neglect of
natural death leaves Hobbes's sovereign exposed to those dissi-
dents who realize that since they face natural death anyway
there are concerns more important to them than the protection from violent death proffered by the sovereign. Becker
assumes that the denial of death is natural and inevitable, and
he does not consider that competition and greed may be a
cause, rather than an effect, of the denial of death.

Fascist literature is effective in identifying as a critical
weakness in Lockean liberalism the avoidance of the subject of
death, which leaves the individual to confront death in isolation and without any societal support. But if the flaw of liberal
social contract theory lies in its exacerbating the individual's
anxiety about death, and in its inability to expect citizens to
risk death for the public good, then the fascists' antidote for

this weakness is not to confront death but rather to obliterate the individual. The theoretical contradictions and racist nonsense of fascism are devoted to lessening one's fear of death and to the sacrifice of life not by looking death in the face but by taking the individual off his lonely and vulnerable pedestal and creating the mythology of perpetual life through the race. Its dependence upon empire and war manifests classically what Robert J. Lifton and Eric Olson describe as the effort to create an illusion of immortality and of power over death by delivering death to other people.[15]

For a similar reason, Marcuse is mistaken in assuming that the modern liberal state maintains its hold over its subjects by preoccupying them with death so as to cement their anxious dependence upon government. To begin with, Marcuse's argument simply flies in the face of overwhelming evidence throughout the burgeoning literature on thanatology that the denial of death has, until very recently, pervaded modern industrial states. Marcuse is quite right in perceiving that an obsessive fear of death would promote dependence on an authoritarian state, but his mistake is in not realizing that anxiety about death is increased by avoidance of the subject rather than by confronting it. In her famous interviews with terminally ill patients, Elizabeth Kübler-Ross discovered that it is only when patients can break through the masquerade of denial often maintained by physicians and family that they can begin to accept their condition and to find an equanimity by emphasizing the quality rather than quantity of their days.[16] Marcuse's linking of the awareness of death and anti-democratic political solutions fails for the same reason the similar conclusions cited above fail. They all miss how acknowledging mortality reasserts the social dimensions of people's lives and the natural basis for pursuing participation in political decisions.

The most direct impact the consciousness of death has upon politics and democratic theory in particular is to bring much-needed new life to the concept of equality. The democratic credentials of death have, of course, always been recognized to some extent. In spite of the well-provisioned send-offs to the nether world historically accorded the rich and the powerful, the unselectivity of death has always been imposing and disruptive of grand human designs to make permanent the sway of any great figure or lineage. But the grudging equality this leveling image of death has inspired has hardly been sufficient to nurture democratic hopes or visions. The equality of threat and vulnerability that Hobbes saw death bestowing upon humankind did not lead him to minimize the inequality he saw between common humanity and people of science, like himself, who could grasp the relation of cause and effect. The equal vulnerability of unequal people pointed for Hobbes not toward democracy but toward the refuge of absolute authoritarianism.

Rather than merely deflating the presumptions of the mighty, the awareness of death has its most important effect upon equality by routing historic assumptions about the "masses." Critics of democracy from Plato to the contemporary revisionists have been encouraged in their adjustment to citizen apathy as a fact of life by the conviction that the masses are not intellectually capable of the insight demanded of participation in politics. The depressing inability of the enlightened philosopher to communicate with the denizens of the cave in Plato's *Republic* is an archetypical portrait of the masses' alleged absorption in *doxa*, in opinions and illusions, and of their incapacity for insight about what is real in life. But the need to come to terms with death, which is every person's destiny, radically challenges this elitist assumption that insight derives only from the deductions of the intellect. To recognize that one is going to die is to move from the world of illusion and to begin to ask questions about the purpose of life and the possibility of human happiness. Nor is there any reason to assume that the average person has any less need to cope with mortality or any less opportunity to learn its lessons than the philosopher. It may be true that the majority of people do not look death in the face, but it is not because they do not have the intellectual capacity. The current movement to combat the denial of death in our culture has been led less by an educated elite than by ordinary, courageous people who felt there was something terribly wrong with the price they were being forced to pay in order to maintain taboos on the subject of death.

It is a striking paradox that the awareness of death, which is avoided by so many lest it rob life of meaning, can provide an escape from the banality of the compulsive acquisitiveness inspired by Lockean liberalism and can help one to discover the satisfaction and richness of one's social existence. The paradoxical connection between vulnerability and self-revelation has an important relation to democracy and a sense of community. In lamenting that American culture has too often sought to deal with social problems by merely expanding its frontier or its economy, William Appleman Williams begins his book, *The Great Evasion*, with a keen insight into how a sense of community must wait upon a recognition of inadequacy: "America's great evasion lies in its manipulation of Nature to avoid a confrontation with the human condition and with the challenge of building a true community."[17]

In a more melancholy, because less prescriptive, fashion, Hannah Arendt ends her profound examination of the preconditions of a public life in *On Revolution* by describing the regret of a young French poet that liberation, for him and his comrades in the Resistance during the Second World War, would mean "liberation from the 'burden' of public business as well." Thus "back they would have to go to the *epaisseur triste* of their private lives and pursuits, to the 'sterile depression' of the prewar years." The treasure the poet had discovered in the Resistance "was that he had 'found himself,' that he no longer suspected himself of 'insincerity,' that he needed no mask and no make-believe to appear, that wherever he went he appeared as he was to others and to himself, that he could afford to go naked."[18]

Williams and Arendt both grasp the powerful force for communal relationships imbedded in the recognition of incompleteness and dependence in the face of adversity. Because they do not relate this insight to human mortality, the cause of an awesome sense of vulnerability for every person, Williams is left uncertain about the chances for a change in people's consciousness, and Arendt is forced to treat the opportunity for self-revelation in public life as both fleeting and limited to a fortunate few. Freedom and public space, which Arendt views as crucial for political life, would not be seen as the privilege of only an esoteric elite like John Adams and his heirs if Arendt could see that everyone has the need to find meaning and support with other people in facing up to their common mortality.

These examples are useful because they lead directly into the third precondition for democracy that is profoundly affected by acknowledging mortality. As forcefully as it facilitates thinking about new possibilities for equality and community, the awareness of death drastically alters previous assumptions about democracy's lacking a starter mechanism that could move society from elitist to democratic institutions without first violating democratic values. Central to the arguments of the pluralist revisionists of democracy is the assumption that the political apathy they see in most people could be dispelled only by simplistic ideological appeals by demagogues. This skepticism about enlightening the masses is only a recent manifestation of a long-standing despair in political theory about popular espousal of public values. Plato's *Republic* is a utopia most significantly because the *demos* could never be expected to have the insight or discipline to make a philosopher their ruler. Even with the origins of the Philosopher Kings' rule left unexplained, Plato sees the producer class embracing the common good only with the influence of myth and conditioning. Even on the other side of the spectrum as regards enlightened citizens, when Rousseau dares to establish his social contract on each citizen's commitment to the general will, this remarkable democracy is possible only after the supremely undemocratic reliance upon the Great Legislator, who must interpret and mold the general will.[19]

In rejecting dependency upon a Great Legislator or other master social engineer, those who also reject the pluralist attempt to scale down expectations of democracy and equality are bedeviled by the dilemma of how to shape popular con-

sciousness democratically. The most creative thinker to wres-
tle recently with this conundrum is C.B. Macpherson in his
brief, important treatise, *The Life and Times of Liberal Democracy*. He sees clearly that "the main problem about participatory democracy is not how to run it but how to reach it." The
first prerequisite for change he sees is a change in people's
consciousness from seeing themselves as essentially consumers to seeing themselves as exerters of their capacities "in
conjunction with others, in some relation of community." The
other prerequisite is "a great reduction of the present social
and economic inequality, since that inequality . . . requires a
nonparticipatory party system to hold the society together."
He acknowledges that these two essential changes catch us up
in a "vicious circle. . . . For it is unlikely that either of these
prerequisite changes could be effected without a great deal
more democratic participation than there is now. The reduction of social and economic inequality is unlikely without
strong democratic action. And it would seem, whether we
follow Mill or Marx, that only through actual involvement in
joint political action can people transcend their consciousness
of themselves as consumers and appropriators. Hence the
vicious circle: we cannot achieve the changes in social inequality and consciousness without a prior increase in democratic participation."[20]

More optimistic than Macpherson, Benjamin Barber observes this same conundrum in noting that "community grows
out of participation and at the same time makes participation
possible."[21] Macpherson makes an imaginative and forceful
attempt to portray how this vicious circle might be broken by
highlighting present weaknesses in the system of consumer
liberalism in delivering according to schedule and in satisfying consumer consciousness. In this regard, Macpherson
speaks of the increasing awareness of the costs of economic
growth in the pollution of air, water, and earth as possibly
taking people beyond sheer consumer consciousness. Other
weak points in the vicious circle that Macpherson finds are
demoralization from lack of democratic participation in the
workplace and the need for corporate capitalism to avoid

breakdown by spreading real goods more widely, thus risking a reduction in social inequality.

Without going into an analysis of the probability of change resulting from these tensions within the stolid status quo of pluralist democracy, it is enough for our purposes to recognize Macpherson's insight in appraising and seeking to cope with the dilemma of democratic change, and to appreciate how much his case for the possibilities of change could be strengthened by taking note of the potential power for altering people's consciousness of a willingness to acknowledge human mortality. One of the most striking results of the awareness of death is how powerfully it affects our priorities and values; it thus can potentially serve as the very catalyst for changing popular consciousness that has eluded democratic theory.

As I have argued in earlier contexts, recognizing our mortality, more than anything else, forces us to acknowledge not only our finiteness but limits in general, and that recognition opens up the chance to see through the smoke screen of unlimited acquisition and the psychologically ruinous pursuit of economic growth for the sake of growth. It is not by accident that a culture that motivates people by self-interest and a lusting to acquire more without any regard to need would also spawn cryogenics and Forest Lawn and make the very subject of death a taboo. As cracks begin to appear in our avoidance of death, however, compulsive acquisition is also threatened because a sense of limits has the great benefit of allowing one to gain perspective and a sense of proportion. Just as the illusion that life is unlimited also devalues life, so the realization of life's limits helps one to value each day and to focus on the human relationships that give joy and meaning to life.

It is important to reemphasize that the movement to deal more honestly with death has progressed in the past decade without the tutelage or scarcely even the awareness of governments or educated elites. The vast change in attitudes toward death, already begun in American society, has been forced by average people who have sensed the psychological costs of maintaining silence about death. These people have insisted as a first step that the dying and the aged not be shunted off in

institutions simply because the infirm clash with our presumptions and preoccupations as consumers. If Rousseau is
correct in seeing the essence of democratic consciousness rest-
ing in a person's ability to respond to issues as a citizen rather
than a maximizer of self-interest, these people have already
taken important steps toward a new democratic consciousness. They see the limits of a political and economic system
based on self-interest, and they see how much we are social
beings whose manner of life and death is vastly affected by the
public values of the society.[22]

It is obviously too early to say how broadly the awareness of
mortality may serve as a catalyst for a new democratic consciousness, but that such an awareness has begun to spread at
all is a momentous development that demands close attention
from political and social theorists. If it is the function of
political theory to perceive new political possibilities and to
explore and articulate alternatives to present restrictions
upon the human need for creativity and community, then there
is an urgent need to take stock of the significant political
ramifications of people's attitudes toward death. Since studies
have found that the subject of death can be as stressful and
fearsome for religious as for nonreligious people,[23] it should be
reasserted that in our pluralistic culture coping with death is
one of the great challenges that unites us and whose lessons
can serve as a unique basis for democratic consensus on what
constitute the priorities of our society. This fact only underlines our social dependency and need of support in honestly
facing life's mysteries. Without much of this support, some
brave people have, nevertheless, begun to confront death can-
didly, and to insist that social values and political goals that
ignore the human need for meaning and creativity in the face
of death are finally worthless, regardless of the prosperity they
offer as a distraction from a sense of vulnerability. If our
society were to develop the customs, symbols, and other cultural reinforcements that supported increasing numbers of
people in acknowledging the fragility of their individual existence and the importance and satisfaction of finding communi-

ty with their fellow mortals, it may not be presumptuous or naive to anticipate a vastly changed political consciousness and vastly raised hopes for participatory democracy.

After examining some of the long-range political consequences of a greater openness to the subject of death in our society, I will now consider an issue that does not allow us the luxury of gradual change: the crisis of the nuclear arms race. Certainly no issue could more severely test and challenge the significance of political changes I have attributed to changing attitudes about death, and no issue stands more in need of the potential of those changes. The largest change that a greater openness to death can make in our nuclear peril is not different from the effect of that openness on the prospects for democracy: the development of a new political consciousness that makes political changes formerly thought impossible now practical and necessary.

8. Accepting Mortality and Rejecting Nuclear Peril

"There's nothing serious in mortality. All is but toys."
—Macbeth

The coming of the nuclear age has been accompanied by a rash of paradoxes. The most prominent and devastating of these is the spectacle of human genius producing at its zenith possible extermination of all human life from this planet. Despite magnificent advances in science and knowledge, we seem piteously unsteady in trying to contain an arms race that threatens total catastrophe. Humanity has never been more learned and more powerful, and it has never been more insecure and more helpless. But the paradox of how accepting our mortality can enrich our lives may provide a basis for hope in the face of the nuclear peril that bedevils our age. Though it is largely overlooked, the threat of nuclear death can change our view of death in general, and a new perspective on mortality might provide humanity with the motivation, courage, and insight required to take concrete steps to avoid nuclear obliteration.

In exploring the link between the acceptance of mortality and the rejection of our present nuclear peril, I focus on the remarkable books by Jonathan Schell, *The Fate of the Earth* and *The Abolition*. Schell's work is widely recognized as possibly the most powerful and influential description to date of the danger and destruction presented by nuclear weapons and the plans for employing them in both East and West. But Schell's books are important not only for their striking insights on the numbing paradoxes of the nuclear arms race but also for an incompleteness and a key mistake when charting a direction away from the "nemesis of all human intentions, actions, and hopes."

Perhaps because of the very precision and astuteness of Schell's description of our present danger, his speculative and general prescriptions in *The Fate of the Earth* for an alternative future—for "reinventing politics"—provoke heated criticism. He seeks to disarm critics by more pragmatic recommendations in *The Abolition*. Yet the imaginative and useful proposals in the second book lack the theoretical grounding and vision of the first book. In its very inadequacies, the second book is a recommendation to reconsider the ideas of the first. Accordingly, I will argue that his ideas in the first book lay a better foundation for the personal and social changes required to stave off the nuclear threat than his critics, and perhaps Schell, realize. The danger of nuclear warfare that Schell describes sheds a wholly new light on individual death and the ability of people to reconcile themselves to mortality. Schell presents a crucial reinforcement for a perspective on death that reaffirms the meaning and power of each person's life. Such a perspective provides vital support for the changes that his critics are too quick to dismiss as implausible.

Schell's first of three chapters, "A Republic of Insects and Grass," is a fearsome and gruesome primer on nuclear weapons and the total devastation wrought by those weapons. Whether relating cold, startling facts—such as that the nuclear nations now possess warheads with the destructive force of 1.6 million times the atomic bomb dropped on Hiroshima— or acquainting his reader with thermal pulses, blast waves, and the three stages of radiation sickness, Schell's treatment of our danger is wholly convincing. One understands immediately the reason for his renown as a writer and why this book represents a watershed in the dawning realization of the extent to which we are endangered by nuclear weapons.

The first chapter takes one through the hell of Hiroshima and the Simple Simon world of strategies for limited nuclear war. It is in the second and third chapters that Schell most directly considers the implications of our attitudes toward

nuclear war and the failure of response to our peril in which
"both self-interest and fellow-feeling seem to have died." He
forces us to realize how completely we passed from an age of
innocence with the onset of nuclear weapons when he makes
the stark point that now we can never escape a universe in
which we have the power to end all life. As far as we are from
dismantling all nuclear weapons and the facilities to build
them, Schell confronts us with the fact that even if the world
were to take these extraordinary, seemingly miraculous steps,
we could still not destroy the scientific knowledge that, with
sufficient provocation, could be used to rebuild the bombs.
This perception that humanity is inescapably stuck with the
danger of its destruction is central to all the arguments and
theories that Schell advances. He is certain that we are in a
new age in which no technological developments or new inventions, the source hitherto of our faith in progress and a better
future, will guarantee us freedom from annihilation. The permanence of the nuclear dilemma obviously adds significantly
to Schell's tone of exasperation and alarm about our indifference to our danger and our wishful confidence that mere
adjustment, and not radical change, is necessary to deal with
the problem of nuclear weapons. Accordingly, before address-
ing the extent of the political and social changes demanded by
our new and permanent peril, Schell seeks to undermine the
smug assumption that we can proceed with business as usual
and to show how pathetically out of date are our attitudes
about war and the justification of international conflict. A
primary target for Schell becomes the strategy of deterrence
upon which the nuclear powers base their security.

Schell believes the concept of deterrence is ineffective in
both theory and practice, and he effectively exposes the lack of
seriousness with which both leaders and their peoples respond
to the nuclear peril. He argues that the logical fault line in the
doctrine of deterrence "runs straight through the center of its
main strategic tenet—the proposition that safety is achieved
by assuring that any nuclear aggressor will be annihilated in a
retaliatory strike." Whereas the doctrine depends for its success on "a nuclear-armed victim's resolve to launch the anni-

hilating and second strike, it can offer no sensible or sane justification for launching it in the event." Schell points out that the logic of prenuclear deterrence was maintained by each side's readiness to wage war and try for victory if deterrence failed. But since nuclear deterrence begins by assuming that victory is impossible, Schell concludes: "Thus, the logic of the deterrence strategy is dissolved by the very event—the first strike—that it is meant to prevent. Once the action begins, the whole doctrine is self-cancelling. In sum, the doctrine is based on a monumental logical mistake: one cannot credibly deter a first strike with a second whose *raison d'être* dissolves the moment the first strike arrives. It follows that, as far as deterrence theory is concerned, there is no reason for either side not to launch a first strike."[1]

Schell's analysis of the practice of deterrence is even more damning than his examination of its logic. Deterrence theory puts a brake on any debate of its adequacy or reasonableness. Precisely because the appearance of credibility is so important to deterrence, states cannot afford to discuss whether one *ought* to retaliate after a first strike. The maintenance of this appearance of credibility of response can also lead nuclear states to be more rigid and aggressive, rather than restrained, in conventional conflicts in order to demonstrate their resolve to uphold their role in the mutual-assured-destruction strategy. Instead of frightening states away from conventional conflicts, it appears that deterrence strategy could exacerbate and escalate the danger of those conflicts as each side seeks to demonstrate its credibility and will.

Schell reminds us that this variance of nuclear deterrence from its stated purpose is not merely a matter of conjecture. Both the United States and the Soviet Union claim that it is only for *survival* that they produce and deploy weapons that portend the possible extinction of humanity, but "the aim of holding on to the system of sovereignty introduces a much less reassuring, much less frequently voiced, and much less defensible proposition, which is that one prepares for extinction in order to protect national interest" (209). Thus, both the United States and Soviet Union identify "vital interests" that they intend to protect, if necessary, even with the use of nuclear weapons. This fact reflects how casual is the drift by nuclear nations from taking responsibility for the survival of the world. We subscribe to deterrence for the sake of survival, but then we find that we are prepared to risk the sacrifice of mankind for our national interests.

Schell argues that our casualness about nuclear arms has serious effects upon us that are masked by the totality of our peril. Beneath our quest for normalcy rumble the two stark realities of our nuclear strategy that we strive desperately to ignore: one, "that at any moment our lives may be taken from us and our world blasted to dust"; and two, that "we are potential mass killers." The heavy moral cost of nuclear armament is that "it makes of all of us underwriters of the slaughter of hundreds of millions of people and the future generations—an action whose utter indefensibility is not altered in the slightest degree by the fact that each side contemplates performing it only in 'retaliation'" (152). Schell also argues that we cannot find exoneration from complicity in the slaughter of humanity in the theoretical justification that we possess nuclear arms, not in order to use them, but in order to prevent their use, for "the fact is that even in theory prevention works only to the degree that it is backed up by the plausible threat of use in certain circumstances." Our pretension at holding life sacred, a conviction we assume to be at the core of our civilization, is exploded in our accepting roles as the victims and perpetrators of nuclear mass slaughter. "Somehow, according to a 'strategic' logic that we cannot understand, it has been judged acceptable for everybody to be killed." (153).

In steeling ourselves against recognizing the moral implications of our nuclear strategy, we pay a price in our personal lives as this indifference to reality and morality trickles down: "In the long run, if we are dull and cold toward life in its entirety we will become dull and cold toward life in its particulars—towards the events of our own daily lives" (148). This is the same trickling down of avoidance and despair that undermines life in society in general: "The society that has accepted the threat of its utter destruction soon finds it hard to react to lesser evils, for a society cannot be at the same time asleep and awake, insane and sane, against life and for life" (152).

Perhaps the most profound price Schell sees us paying in our seeming indifference to the nuclear peril is that we are gradually cutting ourselves off from that "common world," which Hannah Arendt describes as surviving in each person and providing for each person connection and meaning in the human community. In what may be the most moving passage in his book, Schell sees the danger to the common world in the future necessarily diminishing us in the present:

The thought of cutting off life's flow, of amputating this future, is so shocking, so alien to nature, and so contradictory to life's impulse that we can scarcely entertain it before turning away in revulsion and disbelief. The very incredibility of the action protects it from our gaze; our very love of life seems to rush forward to deny that we could do this. But although we block out the awareness of this self-posed threat as best we can, engrossing ourselves in life's richness to blind ourselves to the jeopardy to life, ultimately there is no way that we can remain unaffected by it. For, finally, we know and deeply feel that the ever-shifting, ever-dissolving moments of our mortal lives are sustained and given meaning by the broad stream of life, which bears us along like a force at our backs. Being human, we have, through the establishment of a common world, taken up residence in the enlarged space of past, present, and future, and if we threaten to destroy the future generations we harm ourselves, for the threat we pose to them is carried back to us through the channels of the common world that we all inhabit together. Indeed, "they" are we ourselves, and if their existence is in doubt our present becomes a sadly incomplete affair, like only one word of a poem or one note of a song. Ultimately, it is subhuman. [154-155]

Arendt describes as "radical evil" the crimes that destroy not merely individual victims but the world that in some way can respond to, and in some measure redeem, the deaths suffered. This radical evil of destroying a whole community was what Hitler's effort to exterminate the Jews amounted to and is what the nuclear powers are tinkering with on a larger scale. Schell links genocide and nuclear holocaust as crimes against the future and reminds us that the superpowers *intend*, if nuclear war begins, "to commit genocide against one another—to erase the other side as a culture and as a people from the face of the earth." He also reminds us by this linkage of genocide and nuclear extinction that "insane crimes are not prevented from occurring merely because they are unthinkable" (146). In spite of our attachment to a "normal" world and a sophisticated realism from which we eschew dramatic language like "holocaust" and "extinction," we are jarred by Schell to realize that throughout history, and especially in our own progressive century, the unthinkable has happened.

By the end of his analysis Schell has demolished the arguments of both the so-called realists, who seek security through increasing arms, and the ideologues, who would employ nuclear threats to defend or advance their particular notions of "democracy" and "freedom." His forceful points show how badly the realists need to rethink what they mean by "security." As for the ideologues, he convincingly argues that doom can never be a human purpose because it ends all purposes. He cites the argument of Karl Jaspers in his 1958 book, *The Future of Mankind*, the "life in the sense of existence—individual as well as all life—can be staked and sacrificed for the sake of the life that is worth living." Schell then demonstrates that the flaw in Jaspers's position is that it "depends on an application to the species as a whole of a canon of morality that properly applies only to each individual person." Citing the examples of Socrates and Christ, who saw ethical commandments as absolute for the individual, Schell argues that they represent the conviction that "there are no ethics apart from service to the human community" and that the extinction of the community "can never be an ethical act." (130-31).

The importance and validity of Schell's comments are underscored by a syndicated column by the renowned philosopher Sidney Hook. In response to the alternatives of being "red or dead," which he ascribes to George Kennan, Hook praises Solzhenitsyn's proclamation that some things are more important than mere life, and insists that Americans must be "prepared to stake our lives, if necessary, on freedom." Hook presents the following as his credo:

It is better to be a live jackal than a dead lion—for jackals, not men. Men who have the moral courage to fight intelligently for freedom, and are prepared to die for it, have the best prospects for avoiding the fate both of live jackals and of dead lions. Survival is not the be-all and the end-all of a life worthy of man. Sometimes the worst thing that we can know about a man is that he has survived. Those who say that life is worth living at any cost have already written for themselves an epitaph of infamy, for there is no cause and no person that they will not betray to stay alive. Man's vocation should be the use of the arts of intelligence in behalf of human freedom.[2]

How hollow "the arts of intelligence" and "human freedom" sound after Schell has so persuasively shown that the use of nuclear weapons will be the end of human survival and the end of all other values and goals as well. That someone of Sidney Hook's stature could take a point of individual ethics on survival as a subordinate goal and so obviously misapply it to the society in general and, inevitably in the nuclear age, to all humanity shows how unseriously even scholars can take nuclear war, and how crucial to any discussion about international hostilities is an appreciation of the ideas in Schell's work. If these ideas as we have discussed them are the basis for the extraordinary acclaim for Schell's book, we must yet discuss the book's central problem that has brought vehement criticism, which in some cases drowns out the acclaim. This problem arises when Schell takes up the issue of how civilization might save itself from nuclear devastation, the issue that is the prime concern of his final chapter, "The Quest."

Schell does not present concrete strategies in *The Fate of the Earth* for a way out of the fearsome dangers he describes, and that fact has provoked the wrath of many critics. These criticisms are perhaps more of a tribute to the power of his portrayal of nuclear peril than an indictment of his lack of solutions, since Schell never pretends to offer concrete solutions. He does, however, assure us that the dimensions of dangers we

face are so large and enduring that we must embark immediately on mind-boggling changes that amount to nothing
short of "reinventing politics" or "revolutionizing the politics
of the earth." Precisely because the knowledge to make nuclear
weapons and to destroy the world will be a permanent part of
the human legacy from generation to generation, Schell demands that we face the fact that it is not enough to eliminate
weapons; we must eliminate conflict among nations. He insists
that the "goals of the political revolution are defined by those
of the nuclear revolution," and we must "lay down our arms,
relinquish sovereignty, and found a political system for the
peaceful settlement of international disputes."[3]

If the mere dearth of concrete solutions provoked some
critics, these last words about solutions, which are very general, brought abuse upon Schell from early critics who displayed
a combination of bewilderment and outrage. A *Time* assessment of Schell cited one critic who was distraught that Schell
"hasn't a clue" about the practical problems of disarmament
and that his philosophizing "flirts with the preposterous." The
Time article cited one editorial that accused Schell of "utopi-
anism," and another that criticized him for being "destructive
of serious thought about how to prevent war and control the
spread of nuclear arms" and found ludicrous his calling for
"nothing less than to reinvent politics." Strobe Talbott in *Time*
found Schell's chapter on the way out of nuclearism "by far the
weakest part" of the book and argued that Schell seemed to en-
dorse "simple-minded deafeatism." Max Lerner in the *New Republic* added his conviction that the radicalness of the changes
Schell demands is directly proportional to their shallowness:
"What Schell fails to recognize, enthralled as he is by his
eschatology, is that no plan for averting a nuclear holocaust is
worth anything if it doesn't acknowledge the deeply flawed
nature of man and his institutions."[4]

Even a commentator such as theologian Langdon Gilkey,
who has a fine appreciation for the peril to humanity Schell
describes, finds himself immobilized by the call in the final
chapter to reinvent history: "while 'history as usual' seems to

be insane, nevertheless history not as usual seems to be equally insane."[5] Gilkey contrasts Schell's optimism about the possibilities of change with Robert Heilbroner's somber *Inquiry into the Human Prospect*, published a decade earlier, and notes that Heilbroner seeks to control science, which Schell doesn't think is possible, and Schell seeks to reinvent history and society, which Heilbroner doesn't think is possible.

Gilkey's reference to Heilbroner is instructive, for Heilbroner's treatment of responses to nuclearism embodies the flaw that is found in most of the critics who are dumbfounded by Schell's "apocalyptic" demands for change. The deep melancholy in Heilbroner's analysis stems from the conviction that people will not voluntarily accept the changes and discipline necessary to put an end to dangerous international rivalry; thus, catastrophe can be avoided, if at all, only by authoritative governments terminating freedom and coercing the changes that might save humanity. What I think Heilbroner misses, along with most of Schell's critics, is an insight that moves all of Schell's assessments about what is possible in response to the nuclear peril: the onset of nuclear weapons revolutionized not only our possibilities for destroying ourselves, but also our possibilities for saving ourselves.

Schell's critics accept that there have been qualitative changes in the implements of destruction, but they just assume that the consciousness of human beings is not affected by the dawn of the nuclear age. Schell spends most of his book lamenting that humanity seems so unaware of the threat to its existence posed by nuclear arms, but he seems convinced that the reality of this threat can, quite literally, be brought home to people. At that moment of realization, he expects, old priorities will tumble and a new consciousness will result that can signal a new politics and a new history. What may have seemed a utopian change before nuclear weapons may not seem so now if such a change is our only avenue to survival.

There is, however, a key error in the way Schell develops his argument in the search for a new consciousness, and while this error is not analyzed by his critics, I believe it seriously weakens his case for the possibility of radical change and represents a missed opportunity for Schell to take full advantage of the compelling effects of our nuclear peril.

Schell sees two motives that could compel a general awakening to the dangerous inadequacies of both deterrence and national sovereignty, and the two could compel the development of a new consciousness as to what constitutes "security." The two motives are fear and love. While these motives have traditionally been at odds with each other, he sees them pointing to the same conclusion in the nuclear age:

The "realistic" school of political thinking, on which the present system of deterrence is based, teaches that men, on the whole, pursue their own interests and act according to a law of fear. The "idealistic" school looks on the human ability to show regard for others as fundamental, and is based on what Gandhi called the law of love. . . . Historically, a belief in the necessity of violence has been the hallmark of the credo of the "realist;" however, if one consistently and thoroughly applies the law of fear in nuclear times one is driven not to rely on violence, but to banish it altogether. . . . For today the only way to achieve genuine national defense for any nation is for all nations to give up violence altogether. However, if we had begun with Gandhi's law of love we would have arrived at exactly the same arrangement.[6]

Schell acknowledges that a real difference exists between the motives of love and fear when encompassing the fate of future generations. Because "the law of fear relies on the love of self," this self-love cannot "extend its protection to the future generations, or even get them in view" (224). Love, however, can reach those who would inherit the earth and "can create, cherish, and safeguard what extinction would destroy and shut up in nothingness." Nevertheless, Schell continues to maintain that fear can point the way away from nuclearism: "But in fact there is no need, at least on the practical level, to choose between the law of fear and the law of love, because ultimately they lead to the same destination. It is no more realistic than it is idealistic to destroy the world" (225).

Unfortunately, Schell may well be wrong in this key assessment, and if he is, he not only weakens his case for a possible transition to a demilitarized society, but he misses the opportunity to show how many of his previous points could buttress a wider acceptance of the law of love. The mistake Schell makes at this crucial juncture is failing to see how fear and self-love do not provide a sufficient motive for people now alive to make the hard sacrifices to avoid nuclear doom when such a catastrophe is only a possibility.

Is not self-love the very blinding agent that keeps us absorbed in the moment and that makes us deny the dangers Schell portrays? To the extent that we *do* perceive our danger, would self-love not tempt us to bask in the illusion of power over fate and death that victimization represents? Fearful, selfish people are the least reconciled to their mortality, and might they not, in their resentment and impotence, be the very ones not only to appear casual about nuclear threats in pursuing their personal and national self-interest but also the ones to embrace the bomb? Schell tells us earlier in his book that nuclear war, in one sense, constitutes the perfect crime, because we leave no witnesses to accuse us. He also points out that a nuclear holocaust represents "the death of death"—perhaps a comforting thought to one who finds death the nemesis of his or her self-love. This resentment about the human condition, now highlighted by the nuclear threat, seems exactly what is behind Heilbroner's despair of an indulgent society choosing to make the sacrifices necessary to save itself:

When men can generally acquiesce in, even relish, the destruction of their living contemporaries, when they can regard with indifference or irritation the fate of those who live in slums, not in prison, or starve in lands that have meaning only insofar as they are vacation resorts, why should they be expected to take the painful actions needed to prevent the destruction of future generations whose faces they will never live to see? Worse yet, will they not curse these future generations whose claims to life can be honored only by sacrificing present enjoyments; and will they not, if it comes to a choice, condemn them to nonexistence by choosing the present over the future?[7]

Schell can be forgiven for shrinking from expectations that all of humanity could emulate Gandhi in his devotion to the

law of love, but Schell's mistake is in limiting the response to
nuclearism to the two motives of fear and love and in not
examining how nuclear threat engages concerns of people that
are not as narrow as saving one's skin, or as broad, at least
initially, as loving humanity. In compelling us to face the
vulnerability of our world and of humanity, the nuclear peril
also brings us face to face with our individual vulnerability
and mortality. Increasingly, all people have forced upon them,
with a new relevance and urgency, the need to find meaning
and significance for their lives in the face of inevitable death.
As with the law of fear, the need to find meaning for one's life
affects everyone, but unlike fear it points away from self-interest and, ultimately, locates the significance of one's life in its
impact on the lives of others. In pushing people to face their
mortality and seek meaning for their lives, the nuclear threat
can be a catalyst for the changed consciousness and behavior
that Schell convincingly argues are necessary to counter the
threat.

It is ironic that Schell does not discuss the need to cope with
one's personal mortality as a fulcrum for the vast societal
changes he envisions, though he has previously laid all the
groundwork for this discussion. He sees with great astuteness
how dramatically the threat of universal death changes our
perspective on individual death. If we do not act on the nuclear
peril, our death occurs in a social void and lacks all consolation
and redemption: "When human life itself is overhung with
death, we cannot go peacefully to our individual deaths."[8]

But if we take the nuclear peril seriously in its threat of
extinction, concern about our individual deaths is suddenly
dwarfed and liberated to engage the threat to all humanity. If
we can face down the nuclear peril and control it, Schell
assures us, future generations will "know that their existence
has depended on the wisdom and restraint of a long succession
of generations before them" (171). This comment reminds us
that henceforth life will no longer be automatic, that it must be
skillfully and heroically preserved as a gift from one generation to the next. But there is reciprocity: by "wisdom and
restraint" we give survival to the future generations; they in

turn give back to us the reassurance that our lives and efforts have counted and have not been cancelled out by our individual deaths. Schell says this "inestimable gift to us, passed back from the future into the present, would be the wholeness and meaning of life" (230).

This sense of connection with the future, which inevitably provides an example for connection with our contemporaries, Schell sees as the one positive bequest of the nuclear threat: "For nothing underscores our common humanity as strongly as the peril of extinction does; in fact, on a practical and political plane it establishes that common humanity" (226-27).

Schell makes a mistake in endorsing the possibilities of the law of fear and misses an opportunity to describe fully, for those who are shocked by the extensive social changes he envisions, the powerful relationship of new attitudes toward death and new attitudes toward politics; but he does see with remarkable clarity the vital links between the threat of nuclear death and our response to, in Lifton's words, "plain old death." With Schell's insights and our own imagination, we can see how accepting our personal vulnerability and the sense of connection with our fellow mortals that it underscores provide a solid basis for doggedly seeking to protect humanity in its vulnerability.

Schell's treatment of the response demanded by the nuclear threat creates new paradoxes as well as explicates old ones. Perhaps the most important contribution of *The Fate of the Earth* is found in how well he grasps the lesson contained in the fact that the Chinese character for "crisis" means both "danger" and "opportunity," an ancient paradox that becomes more profound in the nuclear age. But in seeking to portray a more practical way of managing our danger in his follow-up book, *The Abolition*, Schell's vision of the opportunity for human solidarity becomes blurred. The theoretical problems of his second book appear more significant than the practical problems of his first. Curiously, the vital linkage between the personal acceptance of mortality and the rejection of nuclear peril is emphasized as much by the shortcomings of *The Abolition* as by the insights of *The Fate of the Earth*.

The Abolition is characterized by the same clear-headed and moving prose of *The Fate of the Earth*, and yet the objective and arguments of this book are strikingly different. Schell is obviously responding to the critics of his earlier book who found a contradiction between the immediacy of the nuclear peril as he described it and the seemingly utopian character of the solutions he proposed. Schell is unflinchingly pragmatic in *The Abolition* and certainly cannot be accused of being either apocalyptic or utopian. Yet he continues to overlook the danger of nuclear decision makers who cannot deal with their personal mortality and he ignores the potential for practical but dramatic political change in the attitudes with which ordinary people regard death. To the extent to which his earlier work came close to perceiving, and depending on, the power of accepting individual mortality, the new directions in *The Abolition*, although a pragmatic advance on *The Fate of the Earth*, represent a loss of theoretical bearings and a missed opportunity to build further on some valuable foundations in the earlier work.

One of Schell's principal efforts in *The Abolition* is to show that nuclear disarmament is not dependent upon world government. It is the assumption that these two developments are inevitably linked that has scuttled attempts to control atomic weapons since the dawn of the nuclear age. Schell details at length the fate of the Acheson-Lilienthal proposal of 1946 that nuclear activities be placed under international control. The proposal did not solve the political question of how disputes among nations were to be decided, and neither the Americans nor the Soviets were prepared to trust each other. The prospects for control of nuclear weapons were lost in the cynicism that surrounds prospects for international government. While security analysts like Bernard Brodie sought a pragmatic acceptance of political realities in the immediate post-Hiroshima world and rejected the call by Albert Einstein and others for world government, Brodie saw his pragmatism as biding for time while the nuclear question was worked out in a world that would gradually adjust to the eclipse of national sovereignty. Unfortunately, the world adjusted, instead, to ever more dangerous stages of the nuclear arms race, or, as Schell puts it, people lost the vision of a nuclear-free world and accustomed their eyes to darkness.

Because world government was not thought possible, disarmament also was not thought possible. With world government seen as the only avenue to nuclear sanity and with that avenue steadfastly blocked, questions about whether it was acceptable to annihilate whole nations or the whole human race were ruled out of order. We lost not only control over the arms race but also any sense of moral responsibility for it. Schell describes our accommodation to nuclear horror with the syllogism that "there is moral responsibility only where there is choice, but here no choice was seen, and therefore no responsibility was seen either."9

With the issue of limiting national sovereignty vetoing all attempts at nuclear disarmament, Schell's prime purpose now is to demonstrate that disarmament is feasible *without* world government. Ironically, his vehicle for disarmament is a reconceptualized nuclear deterrence, the strategy he inveighed against in *The Fate of the Earth* as being logically and morally contradictory. Even more ironically, the lynch-pin in the rehabilitated deterrence he advocates is the fact that the knowledge of how to construct nuclear weapons is unlosable, a fact that drove him in the earlier book to conclude that humanity could only be safe from destroying itself by ending international conflict and, therefore, by ending national sovereignty. This once-demoralizing fact now becomes the savior of deterrence, national sovereignty, *and* disarmament.

Schell argues that nuclear deterrence, the mutual-assured-destruction strategy, has a vast disproportion between its end and its means. Its end is to maintain the status quo among sovereign nations, but its means is to threaten the obliteration of human life in response to an attempt to break that status quo by the use of nuclear weapons. Humanity is forced to pay an inconceivable price if deterrence fails. Not only is the limited option that deterrence allows intolerable, but instead of discouraging nuclear brinkmanship it has so terrified nuclear strategists that they have deployed more and more powerful

and accurate missiles so that the lead time between a suspected nuclear attack and the decision to unleash the weapons
that will terminate life on this planet is only a few minutes. The
possibility that mixed signals or computer error could initiate
nuclear war is thus horrifyingly enlarged. With the survival of
humanity dangling by such a slender thread, Schell is now
convinced that our only option is not to junk deterrence but to
mitigate its worst features. The worst of those features is the
immediacy with which deterrence requires that the leaders of
the nuclear powers make the decision to seal the doom of
humanity.

Schell is convinced that our situation is so precarious that
we must seek not the improvement of human life but just the
continuation of our world. His goal is to back the superpowers
down the ladder of deterrence so as to win more time before
one side or the other has to confront the choice of capitulation
or suicide. He argues that the unlosable quality of nuclear
knowledge has great value in seeking to encourage the superpowers to risk disarmament, because it assures both sides of
the possibility of rearming and responding to an opponent that
has cheated in disarmament. Rather than prevent the abolition of nuclear weapons, the knowledge of how to rebuild the
weapons is what makes abolition *possible*, for it keeps deterrence in force. With that guarantee as a backdrop, Schell argues that the nuclear powers can begin immediately to scale
down their arsenals toward zero. He argues that the traditional fear of cheating can be met by a concomitant build-up of
weapons that have only a defensive capability. Although defensive weapons as envisioned by the Strategic Defense Initiative
are useless against a fully armed opponent who needs only a
few weapons to penetrate a defensive shield in order to deliver
unacceptable damage, defense systems can be expected to be
effective against the few missiles a cheating power might successfully hide. Thus, since all nuclear powers remain in a
position to rearm and array their defensive forces to protect
this capacity, deterrence continues; but it continues at a level
where days and weeks, rather than minutes, are allowed before
responding to aggression.

Schell seeks by his proposal "not to bring heaven to earth but only to preserve the earth." By suggesting a scenario in which untrusting superpowers can find the time to confirm possible computer errors and to consult their enlightened self-interest, he has contributed invaluably to the debate on nuclear strategies and on the prospects for human survival. But we must consider what may be the costs of Schell's new perspective, now that "not improvement but mere continuation is our dream" (111).

One wants to cheer Schell on in his imaginative attempt to find a practical way to move the world back from the abyss of nuclear devastation. Yet in his effort to move away from the more theoretical *Fate of the Earth,* he loses touch with some keen insights in that work and, therefore, lacks a convincing foundation for several of his key arguments in *The Abolition.* Schell's making peace with the strategy of deterrence is a dramatic reversal, and it is not clear that his earlier devastating arguments against this centerpiece of the pragmatists are not still convincing. It remains true that deterrence depends upon an unflinching nuclear response to an aggressor's nuclear first strike; and yet with that first strike, deterrence has already failed, and it is not obvious why the victims of that attack then should, or would, decide to end all life in hurling back their missiles. This crack in deterrence theory is only enlarged in Schell's less-prepared state of nuclear standoff in which the victim must set about reconstructing nuclear weapons. Would not the logical contradiction in carrying out the dictates of a deterrence strategy that has already failed be only more apparent in those weeks required for response? And would not the ambiguity as to what the victim should do be only a greater temptation to a would-be nuclear aggressor? At the very least, Schell needs to answer his own assault on deterrence in his earlier book.

Schell's new embrace of national sovereignty is another dramatic turnaround that has little rational justification. His pragmatic rejection of the imperative of world government, which he endorsed in his earlier work, certainly makes sense inasmuch as his urgent goal is to begin immediately to reverse the perilous nuclear arms race. Less understandable are the enthusiasm and crudeness of his new aversion to international government, which he feels represents excessive controls from ballooning global institutions, "each one equipped to meddle in some new area of our lives" (87).

Schell seems oblivious to the possibility that international government could centralize those decisions essential to peace and decentralize all others. Similarly, his parallel turnaround on national sovereignty, the nemesis of the first book, goes beyond the demands of a quick start on disarmament. He recants effusively and affirms that "national sovereignty *in itself* is highly desirable" (108). He is inexplicably unmindful of the extreme dangers of manipulative appeals to nationalism and ethnic chauvinism in the nuclear age, dangers he recounted compellingly in the first book. It is one thing to preserve national sovereignty for urgent short-term reasons and quite another to disavow an imposing critique with a pledge of allegiance that is as rationally weak as it is gratuitous.

Schell's unreluctant accommodation to the international status quo brings us to the evasion of his own earlier argument in *The Fate of the Earth* that is the most unfortunate and that relates most significantly to the theme of human mortality. Perhaps the most important insight of his earlier work was how the nuclear age presents not only unprecedented dangers but also unprecedented possibilities and opportunities. He saw this fact applying with special force in our acceptance or rejection of our link with future generations and our need to assure them of a chance for life. He described persuasively the dark effects on us in the present if we ignore our link with the future and the opportunity that link offers not only for renouncing nuclear weapons but for discovering the solidarity with present generations that would make disarmament possible.

Earlier I argued that Schell did not fully articulate how concern for future generations helps one to cope with personal mortality and provides a powerful motive for political change. He certainly was aware in *The Fate of the Earth* of what a catalyst for change a new responsibility for the future can be, yet there is no reliance on that insight in his more realistic book. This is profoundly regrettable, because the influence of the bomb in changing our views on death and community is not an apocalyptic speculation—it is already happening. This change is taking place in the consciousness of the millions of "average" people who refuse simply to accept the madness of the arms race that has been continually escalated by their expert leaders. Around the globe, people are generally out in front of their leaders in sensing the implications of the threat to the future that Schell describes so movingly in *The Fate of the Earth.*

But Schell has moved so far from that topic in his haste to free disarmament from the dead weight of international government that he portrays world leaders as more responsible than his evidence warrants. In arguing that the leaders of the nuclear powers practice more restraint than strategic war-gamers expect, he cites the facts that the U.S.S.R. did not use nuclear weapons against China before the latter had the potential to respond and that Britain did not even threaten the use of nuclear bombs against Argentina in the Falklands War. These examples hardly are manifestations of restraint, inasmuch as the danger from other nuclear powers to the perpetrators would have been extreme. This exaggeration of restraint suggests how far Schell is straining to depend on nuclear "insiders" for enlightened self-interest while ignoring the pressure for change from the untutored multitudes. It is revealing that he makes no mention of the recommendation of the National Security Resources Board that President Harry Truman consider a nuclear attack on the Soviet Union during the darkest days of the Korean War in January 1951. Nor does Schell mention the firm plans of President Dwight Eisenhower's exasperated administration to use nuclear weapons against North Korea if the latter refused to accept a stalemate.

The gap between Schell's optimism about heads of state and his ignoring the growing potential of the mass of people to reject nuclear weapons is important because it underlines that Schell's pragmatic movement toward disarmament lacks a starter mechanism. Schell failed to recognize in *The Fate of the Earth* that leaders who cannot deal with their own mortality lack a sensitivity to the mortality of the world and may even be tempted by a nuclear high. He recognizes more clearly in this book that fear alone is not enough for disarmament: "Fear cannot distinguish between a fire in one's own house and a nuclear holocaust—between one's own death and the end of the world—and is therefore useless even to begin to suggest to us the meaning of the nuclear peril" (5).

But what is it that will get the superpowers to chance peace and the arduous path to disarmament? I suspect that beneath the pragmatist's surface Schell is depending on a significant change in popular consciousness about basic life-and-death issues to spur us toward disarmament. But it is a pity that he does not articulate this dependency and work it into the framework of his argument, instead of repeatedly asserting his contentment with the political status quo. Without relying on a popular change of consciousness that is attuned to our nuclear peril, Schell's momentum for disarmament is left with the same experts who have sought security in the arms race during the last forty years. With a reliance on changing consciousness, he still has a practical proposal that merely takes stock of changes already happening and of a crucial insight in *The Fate of the Earth*: a true realist would hardly accept the incredible danger we face and would not build expectations on a prenuclear mode of thinking. The December 1987 agreement between Mikhail Gorbachev and Ronald Reagan, eliminating 2,400 intermediate and short-range missiles in Europe, marked the first build-down in the history of the nuclear arms race. It is clear that such an initiative toward sanity would not have been possible without a public opinion in both the East and West that was broadly and fervently in favor of nuclear arms reduction.

I do not demean Schell's imaginative effort at a practical solution to the baffling and terrifying arms race. With all of its problems, his proposal brings crucial new ideas to the cause of disarmament and, like his other book, leads the way on a difficult but essential journey that few of his critics have dared to embark upon. But Schell needs to retain more from his first book and needs to blend his theoretical and pragmatic selves. It was an inadequacy in *The Fate of the Earth* that no plan was advanced that addressed the immediacy of the terrible nuclear plight that he so convincingly described. But neither can such a plan stand alone without a theory for how it can be initiated and supported. Schell's proposal for disarmament and a conscious commitment to future generations depend on each other; neither can make it alone. The key omission in *The Abolition* is Schell's vision of how the nuclear peril dramatizes that people need to depend on each other and that our lives make sense only in the context of the life we preserve for others.

Schell's treatment of the nuclear threat, then, is eloquent — testimony to the vital connection between ideas on death and on politics and to the connection between accepting our mortality and sharing life with other people. These connections were central to the most important insights in *The Fate of the Earth* and to the practical problems of *The Abolition*. Appropriately enough in this era of paradoxes, our very survival in the nuclear age increasingly seems dependent on gaining a perspective on death in which we see our individual deaths as far down our scale of concerns, compared to the preservation of the human species. We would then see life extending beyond death in the efforts we make to let others live.

9. The Limits of Self-Interest

> While I thought I was learning how to live, I was
> learning how to die.
> —Leonardo da Vinci

I have argued against the idea that the denial of death is inevitable and natural. I have proposed a perspective in which death is seen as a natural and essential part of life and in which we can affirm our life despite our mortality. The key to this affirmation is the power we have to share life with other people and the fact that we all affect the ebb and tide and indeed the survival of humanity. I have also considered how this perspective clashes with basic assumptions in the ethos of the competitive market society as described by John Locke in the seventeenth century and by Michael Novak in the present. The lure of narcissism in our culture was seen as importantly related to an inability to deal with limits and death. And I have considered the striking difference that accepting death makes in debates about the possibilities of greater democracy and of finding a way out of our nuclear peril. At the end of this journey among both profound skeptics and uneasy visionaries, I step back and appreciate the timeliness of thinking anew about human mortality.

Throughout, I have asserted one central idea: rather than threatening to deprive life of all meaning, death deepens an appreciation of life and the capacity of every person to give life to others. This is no mere cerebral thesis. It is an idea whose implications are as broad as they are urgent and have a force that is emotional as well as logical. Some insightful points that

Glenn Tinder makes about evaluating ideas in his book *Political Thinking* have great relevance: "An idea is living and important only so far as it brings us into relationship with ourselves and with reality, so far as it pulls things together. . . . Feeling necessarily plays a great part in searching for the truth. Much that must be pulled together does not have the definite and conscious form of a fact or an idea. A great idea is one that symbolizes and unifies not only facts and beliefs that are clearly present to consciousness but also intuitions and impulses that have not been focused on and given form. The idea that does this is exciting."[1]

If our intellects have been uneasy with the gaps and avoidances in our traditional treatment of death, our *feelings* have begun to convulse in response to the unsoundness and irrelevance of ideas about life and about death that do not bring the one into relationship with the other. In appreciating the power and excitement in an idea that brings death into phase with attitudes about life, we should look again at how our society both discourages and lays the seedbed for the germination of such ideas.

What has prepared the ground in the feelings and emotions in Western society for new ideas about death and human vulnerability is the emotional toll exacted by the old images we have accepted of both death and life. The old image of death has been horrifying and menacing. The gaunt visage glimpsed has been that of a Grim Reaper whose indifferent scythe is no respecter of seasons and capriciously cuts down new life as well as old. This view of death as the canceler and spoiler of life has forced us to try to hide from and deny death by absorbing ourselves in a peculiar image of life. We have seemed convinced that we could avoid the nightmare by never sleeping, so our image of life could not be a placid one of measured effort and rest but one of a restless contest or quest that demanded all of our energies and commitments to constant activity and growth. Without ever really considering what the point of it all was, we became absorbed in a contest to expand ourselves and those attached to us. In the effort to conquer nature and to surpass in wealth and power as many other people as we could, we felt a respite from the nightmare and a fragile sense of power.

But if our image of death has been a nightmare for us, our image of life that excludes death and achieves power and freedom has become an illusion. With a focus on expanding power and self-interest, modern Western culture since Adam Smith has achieved dazzling economic and technological results. In our increasing enthusiasm for competition for status and celebration of self-interest as the genie that has made possible all of our inventions and conveniences, we have slid into a number of critical oversights. For one, we ignore the unevenness of our splendid inventions and the fact that self-interest can divert our ingenuity into finding new fragrances for the perfume industry or lightweight throw-away cigarette lighters rather than wrestling with a 50 percent drop-out rate in urban schools. In our giddiness about the power of self-interest, we have ignored the point in John Stuart Mill's caution that "one person with a belief is a social power equal to ninety-nine who have only interests."

A classic example of our extravagant expectations of the compensations of self-interest can be seen in a *New York Times* column in which William Safire recites an "Ode to Greed." Always brash and provocative, Safire becomes fervent in this attempt to demonstrate that it is only by exhorting the wealthy to greed that the needy will be effectively helped:

Greed is finally being recognized as a virtue. Dressed in euphemism— "the profit motive" or "growth incentives" or "the entrepreneurial spirit"—our not so deadly sin turns out to be the best engine of betterment known to man.

The world has learned that to concentrate on divying-up diminishes us all, while scrambling to help ourselves helps others; without Greed, there is no wherewithal for Generosity.

By hustling to improve our station, by indulging the desire for necessities that becomes a lust for luxuries, by competing to make our pile bigger, we engage in the great invisible handshake that enlarges pies, lifts all boats and enriches us without impoverishing our neighbor.[2]

It is revealing that Safire rests his case on citing examples of the inefficiencies in state control rather than examples of how the achievements of greed trickle down "[to lift] all boats." The fact is, as in our discussion of John Locke, there is a built-in brake on how much the greed for more in one class can alleviate the needs of another class; for having more, once one gets past necessities and security for the future, is not interesting unless others have less. This is what Edmund Burke meant when he said "the characteristic essence of property . . . is to be *unequal*"[3] and what Ernest Becker was pointing to when he claimed that the allure of gold is that it separates us from other people.

But besides being ineffective as a feeder of the needy, society's unleashing of a "lust for luxuries," which seems so natural and innocuous to Safire and many others, is increasingly disturbing the good-life dreams of those who heed this siren call. Individuals and societies alike, whose singular ambitions are material growth and affluence, are becoming more aware every day of how vulnerable they are to the disillusioned and disaffected people and nations who do not compete successfully. Terrorism is proving a vicious, destructive, and, alas, effective threat for spoilers who are resentful at what they perceive as the avarice and arrogance of these eager accumulators. We are all increasingly hostages to desperate people and their states of mind. Any social theory that today focuses our attention on the interests of those with "the entrepreneurial spirit" and ignores the interests, attitudes—and fury— of everyone else is not only blindly elitist but unrealistic and dangerous.

Quite apart from the state of mind of those who can't compete in the pursuit of "more," however, the celebration of self-interest does perhaps its greatest damage to the states of mind of the very people who buy into this ambition for competition. Adam Smith and William Safire may be right in arguing that competition for a bigger pile increases, however indifferently, the gross national product, but they seem never to consider what it does to the competitors themselves. They celebrate a tragic, Faustian swap of productivity for purpose, of quantity for quality, and, in Mill's terms, of interest for belief. The biggest toll in the invitation to getting and spending is that it forbids us to glance at that limited side of our nature manifested by death, the side that would question the significance of a bigger pile. Unconfronted and unexamined, death is forced to remain as a nightmare that intrudes upon us indirectly but pervasively in feelings of insecurity. This insecurity infects even our most precious relationships. We push our children from the cradle to achieve and excel because we are so unsure of what the future holds for either them or ourselves. Because we are presented with a portrait of human behavior that emphasizes how everyone is trying to get ahead of everyone else, we can rely on no one else for comfort and support.

It is interesting that the one time in life when we come closest to recognizing this insecurity and to questioning our priorities and absorptions is called a mid-life *crisis*. It's called a crisis because we seem to lose our grip and stray from normalcy by abruptly noticing that our individual life is at least half gone and by coming close to admitting the nightmare into our consciousness. In our society enough of us get through this crisis to maintain productivity and Little League championships, but in the process we glimpse what a price individuals pay to maintain "growth incentives" and how our dream of life is not securely insulated from our nightmare of death. As Christopher Lasch makes clear, much of the drive in the culture of narcissism is fueled by a determined avoidance of the subject of aging and death.

Fortunately for us, however, death will not be denied. It continues to assert itself and continues our opportunity to catch sight of how insignificant is the issue of how big our pile is. Of course giving death its due is not the only way of coming to realize the emptiness of a culture built upon greed. One dramatic example of the chaos and weakness of a society where self-interest rules can be seen in the "Crisis Relocation Instructions," published by the Federal Emergency Management Agency. These instructions, meant to be distributed to citizens when our country is on the brink of nuclear war, have provoked much derision for their bizarre tone of normalcy as they advise evacuees to remember to take with them to shelters their insurance policies, wills, credit cards, and post office change-of-address cards. But amid the macabre humor of these instructions are some vital lessons on what any society needs to survive.

One paragraph of the instructions that has been largely ignored by commentators is titled "Postattack Situation." Here citizens receive the following dispassionate reminder: "A major problem in the postattack situation would be the control of exposure to fallout radiation. Yet, to do essential work after a massive nuclear attack, many survivors must be willing to receive much larger radiation doses than are normally permissible. Otherwise work that would be vital to national recovery could not be done."[4]

What is stunning about this statement is that it comes from unsentimental realists who do not shrink from preparing for nuclear war, presumably because nations and people in the "real world" are too self-interested to avert provocation and catastrophe. Yet these realists, who would think it utopian for people to yoke their egos and self-interest to avoid nuclear war, are nevertheless forced to expect people *after* such a war to sacrifice all concern for individual survival on behalf of society's survival. Given the minuscule chances for *any* survivors of "a massive nuclear attack," one can only lament that these realists do not challenge people's egos and short-range interests on behalf of society *before* a nuclear war, the only time they can realistically promote survival.

This example seems to underline both our unexamined acceptance of the rule of self-interest and the realization, by even those most reluctant to acknowledge it, that in crises societies cannot survive if people are not accustomed to transcend their self-interests. There are a variety of circumstances like this in which we can perceive rationally the limits and contradictions in a society's promoting greed and self-interest among its citizens, but at no time are these contradictions more evident, both rationally and emotionally, than when we truly acknowledge our mortality. Face to face with the reality of death, we see and feel the absurdity of finding self-esteem or consolation or refuge in how large our pile of possessions is. In the light, rather than the proverbial shadow, of death, we see the true terms of the bargain offered by an economy driven by greed: the growth and productivity of the system at the expense of the individual's finding meaning in life and acceptance of death. We can hardly wonder why societies that accept the spur of greed should promote the denial and avoidance of death.

Yet the denial of death that has been prevalent for almost a century in our society is already beginning to soften. A burgeoning literature on death and dying, death education classes, the hospice movement, and a greater honesty by physicians with patients are just some of the developments that are pushing our society away from the denial of death. These developments did not have a spontaneous generation but are reminders that, in spite of the imperatives of their economic system, Americans have never bent entirely to the incentives of self-interest. Right alongside the hustling Horatio Algers, promotion-hungry narcissists, and Madison Avenue's push to frantic consumption (perhaps best captured in the ever-youthful beer ad: "Who says you can't have it all?") has been the steadfast resolve of generations of people from all economic strata not to be bought away from some activity that was vital to them. Whoever does something for its intrinsic value as opposed to what or where it can get him or her, whoever delights in anything from Bach to frisbee simply for the enjoyment of the activity puts a crimp in the incentive of greed and is, in some degree, receptive to regarding life in qualitative, rather than quantitative and materialistic, terms. The millions of people who play in community orchestras, who volunteer their time in hospitals, who play recreational sports and can be contented losers, who backpack into nature to find a richness that could never be purchased—these people are evidence that the incentive of greed does not simply own the soul of America. Many of these same people do find a real tension between the unacquisitive side of their lives and their roles in the marketplace as producers and consumers. I do not suggest that people should be angelically devoid of all self-interest, but only that the persistent appeal to greed as the dominant human motivation beckons people to a lonely and artificial obsession. It is not a purpose to live or die for.

Given the mixture of motives in most people's lives, to hope for a greater acceptance of mortality is not to advocate revolution. Rather, it is to build on needs and desires already in people, and to insist that the promotion of unlimited acquisition cannot be allowed to preempt the need everyone has to come to terms with death. The long-range economic fallout of such a priority would hardly be disastrous. The market system would continue to operate, but without the artificial demand for the extraneous and the extravagant, whose only utility is the appearance of superiority they bestow on competitive accumulators. Instead of feeding the illusion that the advantaged people in our society are self-made and have no responsibilities to a larger community, an economy with new qualitative priorities would produce to fulfill human needs across the population rather than concentrating on the privileged elite. It is one of the great self-righteous and blinding myths of that elite that people will work hard and economies will be productive only when there are material, individual rewards for effort and work. Since a crucial part of our liberation from the numbing fear of death is the realization that death does not exterminate us if we give life to others, there are inducements for us to labor more tirelessly and to produce more valuable goods than the incentives of individual economic gain could ever achieve.

A liberation from the fear of death can also point us toward a greater democracy and toward an iron will to put an end to nuclear weapons. With these developments we would not be on our way to a new Jerusalem but would become a society freed from dire threats to its survival in the desperation it has tolerated in the lives of its "losers" and in the hollow prizes it has accorded its alleged "winners." Such a society would not be a utopia, for we would still have to face disasters and disappointments, pathos and tragedy. We would also have to contend with age-old individual inclinations to avarice, pride, and greed. But the big difference is that society would not be cheering on the temptation to egoism; instead it would be concretely reassuring people that such defensiveness is no more necessary than spending our lives hiding from death.

In short, people would be able to relax a bit and feel a calm empowerment in diverting their energies to meet real needs. They would know that death testifies to life's fragility and pain but that it finally does not mock life. They would know that death prods us to value life and our precious power to share life with others.

Afterword

On October 26, 1987, seven weeks after I completed the revised manuscript for this book, our sixteen-year-old daughter, Mari, was in an accident on her way to school and was killed. Since so many of the ideas in this book were inspired by the pleasure and joy I took in Mari's life and that of her brother Joe, I am moved to share two insights forced on me by the experience of losing Mari.

I argue in the book that although death causes enormous grief and pain it does not extinguish the meaning and significance of any person's life. The existence of every one of us affects others' lives, and this spiritual effect ripples through time to all future generations, despite the fact that we die and our bodies return to nature. I have not changed anything in the book in the two months since my daughter's death, and I would certainly not change this central argument. I have a deepened awareness of how cold and cruel fate can be and of how excruciatingly lonely and joyless the world can appear, a condition gentled at times by generous, comforting friends. I nevertheless know viscerally that my daughter remains a part of me and that her life will always affect my priorities and commitments. I do not shrink from the pain that I now know bereaved parents never lose, because the pain is a confirmation of my closeness with my daughter and the continuing evidence of her wonderful spirit. And I know that she will continue in the lives of many friends and family members. Her classmates in a crowded architectual drawing class insist on keeping her stool and drawing table unoccupied. In the future, long after they have perhaps stopped thinking of the shy, perceptive young woman they lost in their senior year, they may make choices that arise from a deeper respect for beauty and humane values because Mari touched their lives at a formative time.

The second insight I have to share is also a point that is treated theoretically in the book but has been seared into my emotions in the aftermath of my daughter's death. I find it incredible that so many people in our society seek fulfillment and meaning in their lives by competing for a larger pile of possessions. The only thing that has allowed my wife and me to bear so far the loss of our child is the conviction that she knew that we loved her and that we know that she loved us. The ideology of quantity, of increase, of winning that one hears so much trumpeted in America today seems piteously irrelevant to the real life events that try people's hearts and souls. I can only conclude that this ideology has no place for people who lose loved ones—that is for the "losers"—and it has no place for death. The significance of the struggle between those who would deny death and and those who would affirm love—and the risk, indeed certainty, of suffering and grief that comes with love—has never seemed more momentous to me than in the last two months. The struggle seems to be about sanity itself. To acquire more and to love less is no protection from death. With a pained vision of a mountain of my own smashed precautions, I know that death will have its way whatever we do. But in spite of the agony and bitter tears it exposes us to, all of my recent education discovers that there is one power that can stand up to death, and that is love.

Kingston, Rhode Island
January 1988

Notes

1. DEATH AS A PARADOX

1. Geoffrey Gorer, "The Pornography of Death," in Edwin S. Schneidman, ed., *Death: Current Perspectives* (Palo Alto, Calif.: Mayfield, 1984), 26-30.

2. A.E. Christ, "Attitudes Toward Death Among a Group of Acute Geriatric Psychiatric Patients," *Journal of Gerontology* 16 (1961): 59; Richard Kalish, "Aged and the Dying Process: The Inevitable Decision," *Journal of Social Issues* 21 (1965): 88.

3. Philippe Aries, "The Reversal of Death: Changes in Attitudes Toward Death in Western Societies," in David E. Stannard, ed., *Death in America* (Philadelphia: University of Pennsylvania Press, 1974), 135.

4. Jessica Mitford, *The American Way of Death* (New York: Simon and Schuster, 1963), 14, 16; Richard G. Dumont and Dennis C. Foss, *The American View of Death: Acceptance or Denial?* (Cambridge: Schenkman, 1972), 39.

5. Robert Blauner, "Death and Social Structure," *Psychiatry* 29 (1966): 391.

6. John S. Stephenson, *Death, Grief, and Mourning: Individual and Social Realities* (New York: Free Press, 1985), 34.

7. Robert Kastenbaum and Ruth Aisenberg, *The Psychology of Death* (New York: Springer, 1976), 194.

8. Ernest Becker, *Escape from Evil* (New York: Free Press, 1975), 124; Glenn Tinder, *Political Thinking* (Boston: Little, Brown, 1986), 5; *New York Times*, 3 February 1981, p. A14.

2. SURMOUNTING THE DENIAL OF DEATH

1. Herman Feifel, "The Meaning of Death in American Society: Implications for Education," in Betty R. Green and Donald P. Irish, eds.,

Death Education: Preparation for Living (Cambridge: Schenkman, 1971), 12; Corliss Lamont, *The Illusion of Immortality* (New York: Frederick Ungar, 1965), 271-72.

2. Charles W. Wahl, "The Fear of Death," in Herman Feifel, ed., *The Meaning of Death* (New York: McGraw-Hill, 1959); Peter Koestenbaum, *The Vitality of Death* (Westport, Conn.: Greenwood, 1971); Leon Kass, "Averting One's Eyes, or Facing the Music?—On Dignity and Death," in Peter Steinfels and Robert M. Veatch, eds., *Death Inside Out* (New York: Harper and Row, 1974); Norman Cousins, *The Celebration of Life: A Dialogue on Immortality and Infinity* (New York: Harper and Row, 1974); H. Tristham Englehardt, "The Counsels of Finitude," in Steinfels and Veatch, *Death Inside Out;* Robert Jay Lifton, "The Sense of Immortality: On Death and the Continuity of Life," in Herman Feifel, ed., *New Meanings of Death* (New York: McGraw-Hill, 1977).

3. Paul Ramsey, "The Indignity of 'Death With Dignity,' " in Steinfels and Veatch, *Death Inside Out,* 96.

4. Vivian Rakoff, "Psychiatric Aspects of Death in America," in Arien Mack, ed., *Death in American Experience* (New York: Schocken, 1973), 150; William F. May, "The Social Power of Death in Contemporary Experience," in Mack, *Death in American Experience,* 103; Robert Fulton and Gilbert Geis, "Death and Social Values," in Robert Fulton, ed., *Death and Identity* (New York: John Wiley, 1965), 68-69; Yeager Hudson, "Death and the Meaning of Life," in Florence M. Hetzler and Austin H. Kutscher, eds., *Philosophical Aspects of Thanatology* (New York: Arno, 1978), 91.

5. Jacques Choron, *Death and Modern Man* (New York: Collier, 1964), 10.

6. Ernest Becker, *The Denial of Death* (New York: Free Press, 1973), 26.

7. Jean Jacques Rousseau, *The Social Contract* (New York: Washington Square, 1967), 7; Otto Rank, *Modern Education: A Critique of Its Fundamental Ideas* (New York: Knopf, 1932), 13; Norman O. Brown, *Life Against Death: The Psychoanalytic Meaning of History* (New York: Viking, 1959), 252; Becker, *Escape from Evil,* 51.

8. Choron, *Death and Modern Man,* 171.

9. Anatole Broyard, "Intimations of Mortality," *New York Times,* 15 January 1978.

10. Choron, *Death and Modern Man,* 173.

11. Hudson, "Death and Meaning," 98.

3. THE DENIAL OF DEATH IN THE NUCLEAR ERA

1. Robert Jay Lifton, *The Broken Connection: On Death and the Continuity of Life* (New York: Simon and Schuster, 1979), 13.

2. Robert Jay Lifton and Richard Falk, *Indefensible Weapons: The Political and Psychological Case Against Nuclearism* (New York: Basic Books, 1982), 65.

3. Hans Morgenthau, "Death in the Nuclear Age," in Nathan A. Scott, ed., *The Modern Vision of Death* (Atlanta: John Knox, 1967), 76.

4. Lifton and Falk, *Indefensible Weapons*, 67.

4. ACCEPTING DEATH: THE BENEFITS
OF HUMAN VULNERABILITY

1. Talcott Parsons, Renee C. Fox, and Victor M. Lidz, "The 'Gift of Life' and Its Reciprocation," in Mack, *Death in American Experience*, 3.

2. Jordan M. Scher, "Death—The Giver of Life," in Hendrick M. Ruitenbeek, ed., *Death: Interpretations* (New York: Dell, 1969), 104; Kass, "Averting One's Eyes," 113; Robert S. Morison, "The Dignity of the Inevitable and Necessary," in Steinfels and Veatch, *Death Inside Out*, 100.

3. Peter Koestenbaum, *Is There an Answer to Death?* (Englewood Cliffs, N.J.: Prentice-Hall, 1976), 11, 13.

4. Victor E. Frankel, *The Doctor and the Soul* (New York: Knopf, 1966), 64.

5. John Fowles, "Human Dissatisfactions," in Shneidman, *Death: Current Perspectives*, 5.

6. Hudson, "Death and Meaning," 97, 98.

7. Paul Tsongas, *Heading Home* (New York: Knopf, 1984), 165-66.

8. Jacques Choron, *Death and Western Thought* (New York: Macmillan, 1963), 15; George Wald, "The Origin of Death," in John D. Roslansky, ed., *The End of Life* (Amsterdam: North-Holland Publishing, 1973), 3,6; Frankel, *Doctor and the Soul*, 69.

9. Hudson, "Death and Meaning," 97.

10. Gerda Lerner, *A Death of One's Own* (Madison: University of Wisconsin Press, 1985), 116.

11. Cousins, *Celebration of Life*, 31.

12. John Hick, *Death and Eternal Life* (New York: Harper and Row, 1976), 152.

13. Choron, *Death and Modern Man*, 86.

14. Krister Stendahl, "Immortality Is Too Much and Too Little," in Roslansky, *End of Life*, 74, 76.

15. John A.T. Robinson, *On Being the Church in the World* (Philadelphia: Westminster, 1960), 133.

16. Cousins, *Celebration of Life*, 14.

17. Abbé Pierre, 1980 Calendar, *The Catholic Worker.*

5. DEATH AND POLITICS: THE CLASH WITH CAPITALISM

1. Hannah Arendt, *On Violence* (New York: Harcourt, Brace and World, 1969), 19; Thomas Hobbes, *Leviathan* (New York: Bobbs-Merrill, 1958), 107.

2. John Locke, *Of Civil Government* (Chicago: Henry Regnery, 1955), 102, emphasis added.

3. Hobbes, *Leviathan*, 177.

4. C.B. Macpherson, *The Political Theory of Possessive Individualism* (London: Oxford University Press, 1962).

5. Locke, *Of Civil Government*, 38.

6. Michael Novak, ed., *Capitalism and Socialism* (Washington: American Enterprise Institute, 1979), 115.

7. Michael Novak, ed., *The Denigration of Capitalism* (Washington: American Enterprise Institute, 1979), 59.

8. *Toward the Future: Catholic Social Thought and the U.S. Economy* (New York: Lay Commission on Catholic Social Teaching and the U.S. Economy, 1984), 21.

9. Michael Novak, *The Spirit of Democratic Capitalism* (New York: Simon and Schuster, 1982), 23.

10. Thomas Fitzgerald, "Why Motivation Theory Won't Work," *Harvard Business Review* (July-August 1971), 43.

11. Novak, *Spirit of Democratic Capitalism*, 94.

12. Milton Friedman, *Capitalism and Freedom* (Chicago: University of Chicago Press, 1981), 133.

6. DEATH AND POLITICS: THE ROAD
TO NARCISSISM AND BACK

1. Daniel Bell, *The Cultural Contradictions of Capitalism* (New York: Basic Books, 1976), 12.

2. Christopher Lasch, *The Culture of Narcissism* (New York: Norton, 1978), 65.

3. Novak, *Spirit of Democratic Capitalism*, 108; Lasch, *Culture of Narcissism*, 71-73.

7. DEATH AND ENLIVENING DEMOCRACY

1. Ted Rosenthal, "How Could I Not Be Among You?" in Shneidman, *Death: Current Perspectives*, 532.

2. Joseph Schumpeter, *Capitalism, Socialism, and Democracy* (New York: Harper and Row, 1962), 269.

3. Among the most significant studies in this area are: Bernard R. Berelson, Paul F. Lazarsfeld, and William N. McPhee, *Voting* (Chicago: University of Chicago Press, 1954); Robert A. Dahl, *A Preface to Democratic Theory* (Chicago: University of Chicago Press, 1956); Robert A. Dahl, *Who Governs?* (New Haven: Yale University Press, 1961); Angus Campbell et al., *The American Voter* (New York: John Wiley, 1960); Gabriel A. Almond and Sidney Verba, *The Civic Culture* (Princeton: Princeton University Press, 1963). For a description of the confusion surrounding the identification of the sources of "traditional" democracy, see Carole Pateman, *Participation and Democratic Theory* (Cambridge: Cambridge University Press, 1970), 16-21.

4. Berelson, Lazarsfeld, and McPhee, *Voting*, 314-15.

5. Almond and Verba, *Civic Culture*, 433-505.

6. Peter Bachrach and Morton S. Baratz, "Two Faces of Power," *American Political Science Review* 56 (December 1962): 947-52.

7. Jack L. Walker, "A Critique of the Elitist Theory of Democracy," *American Political Science Review* 60 (June 1966): 285-95; Robert A. Dahl, "Further Reflections on 'The Elitist Theory of Democracy,'" *American Political Science Review* 60 (June 1966): 296-305.

8. Pateman, *Participation and Democratic Theory*, 16-21; Peter Bachrach, *The Theory of Democratic Elitism* (Boston: Little, Brown, 1967); Benjamin R. Barber, *Strong Democracy: Participatory Politics for a New Age* (Berkeley: University of California Press, 1984), 154.

9. Mulford O. Sibley, *Technology and Utopian Thought* (Minneapolis: Burgess Publishing, 1971), 47.

10. Samuel Bowles and Herbert Gintis, *Democracy and Capitalism* (New York: Basic Books, 1986), 64; Barber, *Strong Democracy*, 144; Dahl, *Who Governs?* 224.

11. Hannah Arendt, *On Revolution* (New York: Viking, 1963), 136.

12. Robert Heilbroner, *An Inquiry into the Human Prospect* (New York: Norton, 1974), 110, 141.

13. Herbert Marcuse, "The Ideology of Death," in Feifel, *Meaning of Death*, 68-70.

14. Benito Mussolini, "The Doctrine of Fascism," in John Somerville and Ronald E. Santoni, eds., *Social and Political Philosophy* (Garden City, N.Y.: Doubleday, 1963), 440, 430; Alfred Rocco, "The Political Doctrine of Fascism," in Henry S. Kariel, ed., *Sources in Twentieth-Century Political Thought* (New York: Free Press, 1964), 114.

15. "This whole totalizing and victimizing process can be seen as a kind of counterfeit immortality. It achieves for one's own group a sense of being elevated above the threshold of death only by reducing the status of another group: One man's immortality is bought at the cost of another's." Robert Jay Lifton and Eric Olson, *Living and Dying* (London: Wildwood House, 1974), 102-03.

16. Elizabeth Kübler-Ross, *On Death and Dying* (New York: Macmillan, 1970).

17. William Appleman Williams, *The Great Evasion* (New York: Franklin Watts, 1974), 12.

18. Arendt, *On Revolution*, 284-85.

19. "He who dares undertake to give institutions to a nation ought to feel himself capable, as it were, of changing human nature; of transforming every individual, who in himself is a complete and independent whole, into part of a greater whole, from which he receives in some manner his life and his being." Rousseau, *Social Contract*, 43.

20. C.B. Macpherson, *The Life and Times of Liberal Democracy* (Oxford: Oxford University Press, 1977), 98-100.

21. Barber, *Strong Democracy*, 152.

22. For accounts of the perspectives of terminally ill patients, see Cicely Saunders, *Care of the Dying* (London: Macmillan, 1959); Elizabeth Kübler-Ross, ed., *Death: The Final Stage of Growth* (Englewood Cliffs, N.J.: Prentice-Hall, 1975), 117-44.

23. Herman Feifel, "Attitudes Toward Death," in Feifel, *Meaning of Death*, 122.

8. ACCEPTING MORTALITY AND REJECTING NUCLEAR PERIL

1. Jonathan Schell, *The Fate of the Earth* (New York: Avon, 1982), 201-02.

2. *Providence Journal,* 13 May 1983, p. A14.

3. Schell, *Fate of the Earth,* 225.

4. "Second Thoughts on Schell," *Time,* 3 May 1982, p. 79; Strobe Talbott, "A Grim Manifesto on Nuclear War," *Time,* 19 April 1983, pp. 20-21; Max Lerner, "Visions of the Apocalypse," *The New Republic,* 28 April 1982, p. 28.

5. Langdon Gilkey, "Thinking About the Unthinkable," *University of Chicago Magazine* (Fall 1983), 7.

6. Schell, *Fate of the Earth,* 224.

7. Robert Heilbroner, *An Inquiry into the Human Prospect* (New York: Norton, 1980), 165.

8. Schell, *Fate of the Earth,* 166.

9. Jonathan Schell, *The Abolition* (New York: Knopf, 1984), 89.

9. THE LIMITS OF SELF-INTEREST

1. Tinder, *Political Thinking,* 6.

2. William Safire, "Ode to Greed," *New York Times,* 5 January 1986, p. E19.

3. Edmund Burke, "Reflections on the Revolution in France," in Michael Curtis, *The Great Political Theories,* vol. 2 (New York: Avon, 1981), 56.

4. Federal Emergency Management Agency, "Crisis Relocation Instructions for Washington County, Rhode Island," 14.

Index